P9-DZZ-533

LIFE-CENTERING EDUCATION
Edward G. Olsen
Phillip A. Clark

The challenge of the future is the challenge to expand the horizons of American education. The futurist goals of life-centered education demand curriculum change, not for the sake of change but for the sake of relevancy. This book can become an outstanding tool for implementing a progressive curriculum designed for America's Third Century.

William Van Til, Coffman Distinguished Professor in Education at Indiana State University, who contributed the Introduction for this book, writes, "*Life-Centering Education* by Edward G. Olsen and Phillip A. Clark is an earnest and eloquent book. It is a call to action on the crucial problem of developing a functional youth curriculum. The authors are established leaders in community education. Their book is a genuine contribution to the debate over achieving a relevant and meaningful curriculum which is going on in America today."

Life-Centering Education will surprise you, fascinate you and challenge you. We can endorse no other book that so dramatically enlarges the reader's vision of the education horizon. For personal reading, for seminar discussion, for implementing a progressive course of study . . . Olsen and Clark's *Life-Centering Education* is highly recommended!

ISBN 0-87812-129-3 Cloth
LC 75-43142
© 1977

$7.95
205 pp.

LIFE-CENTERING EDUCATION

LIFE-CENTERING EDUCATION

by

EDWARD G. OLSEN

Professor Emeritus of Education
California State University

and

PHILLIP A. CLARK

Associate Professor of
Educational Administration
Director, Center for Community Education
University of Florida

PENDELL
PUBLISHING
COMPANY

International Standard Book Number: 0-87812-129-3
Library of Congress Catalog Card Number: 75-43142

Pendell Publishing Company
Midland, Michigan

Published 1977
Printed in the United States of America

with gratitude to our parents

Gustav and Emma Olsen

Truman and Mildred Clark

appreciation of our wives

Pauline Walsh Olsen

Carol Kline Clark

and confidence in our children

Marvin Elliott Olsen
Marcia Olsen Kolar
Douglas Walsh Olsen

David Truman Clark
Christine Ann Clark

CONTENTS

LIST OF FIGURES

OVERVIEW

Life-Centering Education by Edward G. Olsen and Phillip A. Clark is an earnest and eloquent book. It is a call to action on the crucial problem of developing a functional life-concerns curriculum. The authors are established leaders in community education. Their book is a genuine contribution to the debate which is going on in America today over achieving a relevant and meaningful curriculum.

Life-Centering Education proposes "a functional plan for sequential, cumulative and realistic individual and group learning experiences based on the fact that there is only one species of human on our planet, and that this is indeed an endangered species." The book proposes a curriculum based upon enduring life concerns and related problems of living. The authors believe that "with the discipline subjects as resource areas and with personal interests as immediate motivators, this emerging approach to the issue of effective curriculum framework is our best hope for creating truly functional education as a process and a program. Until the heart of the curriculum is essentially life centered, we will not have achieved true community education."

This book will be useful to a variety of theoreticians and practitioners. For instance, community educators will appreciate its comprehensive history and critique of the community education movement. Curriculum workers will find useful its description of life-centered education. The philosophically oriented will find the review of the foundations of western civilization to be especially provocative to them. The historically minded will respect the comprehensive overview of the development of the community school and the emergence of the community education movement which followed. The educational generalists will find that the book's criticism of the academic school is as telling as that of the compassionate critics who have been fostering the alternative school movement.

In Chapter One, "Our Tumultuous Times," the authors consider the rationalism of Greece, the legalism of Rome, and the ethics of Israel. The reader soon learns that the authors do not equivocate. They believe that in our scientific achievements we have entered the nuclear space age. They point out that in our intergroup human relations we are still barbarians. They regard democracy as on trial for its life. The new frontier, they say, is futuristic planning.

In Chapter Two, "Schools in Crisis," the authors develop an unsparing analysis of the inadequacy of an education based simply on the conventional academic subjects. Schools which simply tinker with the curriculum will not suffice.

To the authors, the community school was a substantial step toward life-like education. Chapter Three, "Historic Perspective," sketches the emergence of the contemporary community education movement out of earlier beginnings and is especially perceptive.

Recognizing that there are many current misconceptions of the community education movement which require refutation, the authors discuss in Chapter Four varied misinterpretations and venture their own definition of community education. They see community education as a philosophic concept which can be put into actual operation. Its purpose is to serve the entire community and the larger society. It necessitates involvement by community members and the opportunity for citizens to participate in learning experiences based upon wants and needs. The authors call for institutional and agency coordination and for community problem-solving through the use of all community resources. In this chapter, titled "Community Education: Present and Future," clarification is achieved.

Nor are the authors uncritical of community education. In Chapter Five, "Life-Concerns Curriculum," they take community educators to task for not sufficiently emphasizing the importance of a life-centered curriculum. The community education movement will not achieve its high goals unless it stresses a more meaningful curriculum; thus, the rationale for the life-centered curriculum is set forth. Possible objections to such a program are specified and then refuted. The elements which make up life-centered education are described.

But the authors know that curriculum theory cannot stand alone. It must be accompanied by a workable process of change through educational leadership. Chapter Six, "Leadership for Curriculum Change," carefully describes the various roles which school and community leaders can play in moving toward a more functional and germane curriculum.

Then they sketch in Chapter Seven, "Resources for Curriculum Change," how the many existing institutional resources might function more effectively, and list numerous specific suggestions for advance and improvement.

The book concludes with a challenge "It's Up to Us."

Life-Centering Education is a refreshing book, especially in our time when many educators apparently follow the barometer theory — that is, they simply react to pressures. The conviction of the authors is that the curriculum must focus on basic life-concern activities. A number of these areas of living essential for the development of personal and community competence are set forth:

Securing food and shelter
Protecting life and health
Controlling the environment
Utilizing leisure time

- Communicating ideas and feelings
- Adjusting to other people
- Satisfying sexual desires
- Enriching family living
- Rearing children
- Securing education
- Sharing in citizenship
- Enjoying beauty
- Appreciating the past
- Meeting religious needs
- Finding personal identity
- Adjusting to change
- Growing old, facing death.

The reader who knows the history of curriculum development in America will recognize the kinship of these areas of concern to earlier formulations of functions of living by such theorists as Hollis Caswell and Henry Harap whose ideas led to curriculum experimentation by state departments of education in Virginia and Mississippi during the 1930s. *Life-Centering Education,* however, clearly intends that a functions-of-living curriculum help people deal with the social problems which grow out of major life activities. The authors believe that rooted in such life concerns are our contemporary issues such as "the problems of environmental degradation, overpopulation, malnutrition, disease, exploitation, racism, sexism, materialism, militarism, war, authority, power, social change, and the like." They support a curriculum which deals not only with "enduring life concerns" but also with "related problems of living." Thus their views are consonant with the community education movement which succeeded the overly child-centered progressivism which they rightly consider inadequate.

Paramount in *Life-Centering Education* is a deep concern for dealing freshly and creatively with the social realities of our times — the problems and perplexities which are currently troubling humanity. Yet the book avoids the trap of curriculum oversimplification. For it is clear that the authors are well aware of the importance of values, of the needs of the learner, and of utilizing relevant knowledge.

In a time of major social change when curriculum is widely debated, the authors of *Life-Centering Education* are willing to speak out and advance a proposal. Their viewpoint is worthy of careful consideration.

William Van Til

Coffman Distinguished Professor in Education
Indiana State University

WRITERS TO READERS

As we enter the third century of this nation and the last two decades of the twentieth century, we find ourselves in an exciting, yet troubled, era of continuing confusion, turmoil, and crisis throughout the world. Most everywhere on this planet people are yearning blindly for a better tomorrow but are skeptical of its coming. At the same time, education, a mainstay of the American dream since our nation's founding, is very much in crisis. "What can we do to get a better education?" is the rising cry, the urgent demand made with increasing insistence across the nation. Some critics respond by saying, "We should get back to the basics and do away with educational fads, frills, and student freedoms!" "Teachers are overpaid and underworked!" "The old school was good enough for me and it's good enough for kids today." Others answer, "You cannot go back again — all life is different now. The old traditional school simply does not work in these new times. Instead of trying to go back to what once was, let us drive ahead to what should be!"

The taken-for-granted 2 by 4 by 6 by 9 concept of schooling is simply inadequate for our current needs and for the society that is yet to be. The old idea that education is something secured between the two covers of a textbook, within the four walls of the classroom, during the six hours of the day and in the nine months of the school year is not sufficient. Education should be what we want it to be, rather than what it has been.

Sixty years ago Bertrand Russell well expressed this concern when he observed that "It is because modern education is so seldom inspired by a great hope that it so seldom achieves a great result . . . . (Education) should be inspired . . . by a shining vision of the society that is to be, of the triumphs that thought will achieve in the time to come . . . . Those who are taught in this spirit will be filled with life and hope and joy, able to bear their part in bringing to mankind a future less somber than the past, with faith in the glory that human effort can create."

We believe the central focus of our formal education institutions should be on *improving the quality of human living*. The social, psychological, and economic and political changes of our era demand the kind of education that can really help to improve the quality of living of each individual and also build a better world for all. We are convinced that quality education must include curricula that are oriented to the future, yet ever aware of the past in its relation to present human needs. Such curricula must be neither book-centered, nor child-centered, but rather be life-centered. These curricula should focus directly and sequentially upon the persisting concerns, issues, values, needs, and resources of the human struggle for better living, as seen through ages past and now as we near the twenty-first century.

Life-Centering Education is an examination of community education and the application of this developing concept to curricula of our educational institutions. Fundamental to our ideas is the belief that schools and colleges have three major reasons for being maintained in a democratic society: 1) to help transmit to each new generation the best of the human intellectual-aesthetic-ethical heritage; 2) to help prepare individuals for personally satisfying, successful, and creative living now and in the future; and 3) to help provide society's educative basis for continuing human advance.

Throughout *Life-Centering Education,* we attempt to build historical and conceptual framework for community education and life-centered curricula. We present in this writing some ideas about the direction and scope of our American educational institutions, in light of the tumultuous times we live in and the world society that is yet to be. Our major focus is on the need for significant curriculum change, suggesting that the life processes and concerns of people become the common core of systematic learning of youth — with built-in flexibility to function with persons of all ages, kinds of interests, and abilities. The ideas and suggestions we make are all based upon the central assumptions that: 1) all life educates, not just the school; 2) the goal of community education is to educate people better for better living, for a better world; 3) the school must often lead the community into cooperative development of educational policies and programs; and 4) the major concerns of life today and tomorrow should become the core of the curriculum.

All of the views we offer, however, are of little value without sophisticated leadership for implementation. Consequently, we have devoted a portion of this book to pragmatic ways and means to facilitate curriculum change. We recognize that such leadership can range from slight modification in programs to creating anarchy and rebuilding from the rubble. We have, however, tried to be realistic and recognize that leadership will be most effective when it is gradual, yet continuous, and is built upon the best of our current curricular endeavors. The challenge of reconstructing a system of education from the building blocks of our current system is not only difficult but also requires leadership which vests the goals, direction and creative thinking in the people involved, rather than in status leaders. Such leadership insures continuity and utilizes the diverseness among group members to facilitate desired changes.

Unfortunately, significant social change is often perceived as a kind of personal threat; yet, in our candid moments we realize that no society, community, school or college ever stands still. Confronted by the ever-changing educational needs of our times, we have the opportunity to *ignore change* by personally avoiding getting involved, *resist change* by digging in our heels to keep things the way they are, *accept change* by passively

Edward G. Olsen *Phillip A. Clark*

About the Authors

Edward G. Olsen, Professor Emeritus of Education, California State University, Hayward, is a nationally recognized authority on Community School and Multiculture Education.

During the past forty years, Dr. Olsen has taught, lectured, conducted workshops, seminars and courses in these fields in universities and school districts in Oregon, Washington, California, Montana, Michigan, Illinois, Maine, Virginia, Georgia, Texas and Arizona.

Now retired, Dr. Olsen retains his interest in Community Education; serving as a book reviewer, and as a speaker and discussion leader on community education at professional conferences throughout the country.

Phillip A. Clark is currently Associate Professor of Educational Administration and Director of the Center for Community Education, College of Education, University of Florida, Gainesville, Florida.

Dr. Clark has served in several educational capacities including public school teacher and administrator, community education supervisor, leadership camp director, university student teacher placement coordinator and associate director of the Community Education Center at Western Michigan University, Kalamazoo. He has also provided leadership in the International Association of Community Educators, National Community Education Association, Florida Association for Community Education and Phi Delta Kappa.

making the best of a given situation, or *assist needed change* by committing ourselves to directing that change.

Life-Centering Education has been written as an aid to those persons who desire to assist positive change in our system of education.

Brookings, Oregon *Gainsville, Florida*

ACKNOWLEDGEMENTS AND THANKS

To our teachers, colleagues, and students through years past who stimulated and sharpened our ideas,
To the "Brainstorming Sessions" participants who reacted creatively,
To Willie Brennon, Larry Horyna, Gladys Kimbrough, Marilyn Lavitt, Maurice Seay and A. L. Stefurak, who critiqued this book in manuscript and helpfully offered numerous important suggestions for its improvement,
To Marvin Olsen who reviewed Chapter One critically and effectively,
To William Van Til for his generous and specific overview,
To our competently critical wives who worked endless hours reacting to various drafts of the manuscript,
To the publishers footnoted herein who permitted inclusion of varied materials,
And to Janis Johnston, who typed the manuscript with care, imagination and dispatch,

we are grateful!

1. OUR TUMULTUOUS TIMES

It is no longer sufficient for Johnny to understand the past. It is not even enough for him to understand the present, for the here-and-now environment will soon vanish. Johnny must learn to anticipate the directions and rate of change. He must, to put it technically, learn to make repeated, probabilistic, increasingly long-range assumptions about the future. And so must Johnny's teachers. . . .

Such a movement will have to pursue three objectives: to transform the organizational structure of our educational system, to revolutionize its curriculum, and to encourage a more future-focused orientation. It must begin by asking root questions about the status quo.

— Alvin Toffler, *Future Shock*

If you had lived for a thousand years, you might never have found a time more exciting than our twentieth century — an era of continuing confusion, turmoil, and crisis throughout the entire world. Everywhere on this planet there are people who are troubled and fearful, bewildered and cynical, yearning blindly for a better tomorrow but skeptical of its coming. A generation ago Walter Lippmann wrote that "Our ancestors were sure they knew their way from birth through all eternity, while we are worried about what will happen day after tomorrow." If he were writing today what might he say?

In this nation, as in many others, there is a growing crisis of public confidence, a general feeling among people of all ages and backgrounds that things are fast getting out of hand. *Basic social issues* seem overwhelming: environmental pollution, ecological destruction, population explosion, international conflicts, decaying cities, ethnic prejudice and discrimination, religious warfare, waste of natural and human resources, and the ever-ominous threat of nuclear annihilation. Such fundamental issues are often root causes of more *immediate burning issues:* inflation, increasing crime, energy shortages, political corruption on high levels, underemployment, consumer exploitation, alienation, social fragmentation, attacks on civil liberties, misuse of police powers, and so on. Basic issues and burning issues (a distinction made by the Santa Barbara Center for the Study of Democratic Institutions) are of course closely related, yet the difference between them is crucial for those seeking to design realistic and effective curricula for the years ahead. The Center has said it well:

> If burning issues were really to be resolved — not just faced — they had to be understood. The explanatory power of working on the basic issues through study, reflection, dialogue, and publication could lead to understanding. It might even lead, on occasion, to some practical wisdom about what must be done.[1]

CRITICAL ERA

Affluent Americans generally live in suburbs of physical comfort, yet their upward striving often produces emotional insecurity. Poor Americans typically are economically confined in urban and rural ghettos of material deprivation and psychic mutilation. The older Western world's foundations of general belief in order, reason, and progress — and the confidence that must exist to sustain them — are eroding. Throughout the land there is a widening disbelief in anything that any political leader of any party at any governmental level says about either the burning, or the basic, issues of our time. Similar skepticism surrounds large corporate business and, to lesser extent, labor, academic and religious organizations. Public trust in all our institutions is in steady decline.

Henry Steele Commanger says that "the American people are disillusioned, confused, cynical, and bankrupt in political leadership, political ideas and political morality." In the summer of 1975 pollster Lou Harris announced data indicating that 61 percent of our citizens believe the past decade has made America a worse place to live, and that 72 percent of the population feels the United States is headed in the wrong direction.

We can almost feel the growth of a civic cynicism which produces deep political and social indifference and which can lead toward ultimate ruin.

An ominous sign of our times is that a significant number of Americans have come to believe that democracy has failed, that our social system is beyond repair, and that they, and the entire world, will soon choke themselves in foul air, poison themselves with filthy water, starve themselves for corporate profits, and probably vanish in nuclear holocaust. These critics perhaps reflect historian Arnold Toynbee's documentation that in past centuries numerous previous civilizations rose to power and glory, then declined and disappeared into the dusty pages of history because, Toynbee believed, emergent conditions confronted them with challenges which they could not or would not meet through change. They clung too long to the old, and they died.

To many thoughtful observers today the whole historic framework of our society seems threatened. Responsible, successful, secure and normally optimistic business leaders are privately asking such questions as these:

Can a democratic form of government last much longer in the United States?

With increasing populism and a pluralistic democracy, can a free-enterprise or free-market system survive?

Can the existing private, non-profit sector — including the universities and colleges — survive much longer under the pressures of inflation, competition, and threatened legislative action?[2]

In his quietly disturbing little book, *An Inquiry Into the Human Prospect,* economist Robert L. Heilbroner regretfully observes the spreading loss of confidence that social problems can be solved rationally. He finds three dangerously developing threats to our survival: "Runaway populations, obliterative war, and potential environment collapse." These threats can be seen, he says, "as an extended and growing crisis induced by the advent of a command over natural processes and forces that far exceeds the reach of our present mechanisms of social control." The only long-term solution, he believes, is "nothing less than the gradual abandonment of the lethal techniques, the uncongenial lifeways, and the dangerous mentality of industrial civilization itself." Dubious of success as he is, Heilbroner does conclude that "It is not an inevitable doomsday toward which we are headed, although the risk of enormous catastrophes exists. The prospect is better viewed as a formidable array of challenges that must be overcome before human survival is assured, before we can move *beyond doomsday*." Repeatedly he emphasizes that "all the dangers . . . are *social* problems, originating in human behavior and capable of amelioration by the alteration of that behavior. Thus the full measure of the human prospect must go beyond an appraisal of the seriousness of these problems to an estimate of the likelihood of mounting a response adequate to them . . ."[3]

That response is imperative *now*. It requires both short- and long-range futuristic imagination, decisive thinking, and effective planning on the part of many men and women in many walks of life and by fast-increasing numbers of youth still in schools and colleges. Educators share deeply in this grave responsibility. They must learn to use the full educative process to develop in all students a concerned awareness of "the human prospect" in terms of its hazards, resources, and opportunities.

Demandingly obvious is our insistent need to develop a new curriculum based upon the inescapable fact that the survival of humankind is threatened as never before, and that we must discover how to create practical ways of living humanely together as one family of people in a culturally pluralist world existing precariously on this little Spaceship Earth.

Meanwhile we may expect that during the coming decades millions of America's college, high school, and middle school youth will become alienated from traditional values and patterns of American life. Perhaps they *should* be alienated from our society's obsessions with material things, economic growth, status symbols, power and money, and cults of violence, racism and nationalism. They might then become attuned to newer value systems and life styles essential for the new age: the socially moral requirements of universal human empathy, limitations upon human growth, sweeping transformation of present modes of production and distribution of goods and services, drastic reduction in population, development of world political authority, and the like.

In this spirit we can share the optimism of economist Kenneth E. Boulding:

> In spite of the dangers, it is a wonder age to live in, and I would not wish to be born in any other time. The wonderful and precious thing about the present moment is that there is still time — the Bomb hasn't gone off, the population explosion may be caught, the technological problem can, perhaps, be solved. If the human race is to survive, however, it will have to change more in its ways of thinking in the next twenty-five years than it has done in the last twenty-five thousand.[4]

In this critical era many thoughtful people, including the young, are searching for new definitions of personal meaning and effective ways of extending that meaning to society. That search is our hope for the future. In a limited sense, of course, every age is a critical age. Looking back on Western civilization we identify a number of historic landmarks pointing out the zigzag course of human advance and retrogression. Such periods were the Golden Age of Greece; the coming of the barbarians and the final fall of Rome; the intellectually stagnant Dark Ages; then the Renaissance, the Reformation, and the Counter-Reformation; the democratic political revolutions of the eighteenth century, and the industrial and economic revolutions of the nineteenth century. In our own civilized century, as never before in all history, the good green earth has been red with blood, wet with tears, and hollowed with the graves of many millions. With unprecedented speed, some social orders have been destroyed, others created, and people almost everywhere have been forced into changing value systems and patterns of life.

To be sure, many upheavals of the past were momentous in their day. But all of them were small-scale events in comparison with those of our times. They were small-scale precisely because they usually began undramatically, were largely unheralded at the time, and almost unknown at a distance.

Their growth was slow and initially hardly touched most of the human race. Only imperceptibly, and over much time, did they influence the daily lives of ordinary people outside their regional areas. But, in today's highly interdependent world, it is almost literally true that the life of every person on the planet is caught within the web of often ominous social forces.

Never in the whole history of humanity have world-wide events, movements and disasters crowded so hard upon each other as in these past few decades. So short in time, so fast and so vast in impact! What a time in which to live and to teach! If only people in general and educators in particular can be fully alert to its positive opportunities as well as to its potentially devastating hazards!

FOUNDATIONS OF WESTERN CIVILIZATION

Recognition of reality is the first requisite of educational planning, just as it is the first requisite of social and personal health. Unless professions, nations, and individual men and women become mature enough to face frankly their problems and recovery potential, they can hardly hope to find truly effective ways to overcome the causes of their problems. Adequate social diagnosis is the only sound basis for successful social prescription. This is also profoundly true for educational improvement and functional curriculum development. Before we plan processes and programs to help learners comprehend and improve their world, we and they must understand how the basic and burning issues of today are rooted in the historic development of Western civilization and the United States.

No society springs full-blown from a social and cultural void. Every society roots deep in the varied societies and cultures from which it developed — borrowing some social practices from one, assimilating values from another, transforming traditions from yet a third. Through these cross-societal influences and borrowings, the emerging new society's essential characteristics are shaped. In this way our American society, like that of Western civilization as a whole, has grown out of an historic past. Three essential foundations of our contemporary value system, all of which began in the ancient world, are the rationalism of Greece, the legalism of Rome, and the ethics of Israel. Together these three foundations still underlie the basic value system of the Western world. We are its products. Largely because of them our behavior in dealing with other people — especially with those who differ from us in race, religion, social class, sexual orientation, or nationality — is modified. And our common life together, our society itself, is now surely in peril, torn by fear and hate, facing possible self-destruction because our awesome technological power is not controlled or utilized for planetary human welfare by reason, law, or ethics.

Figures 1 and 2 depict graphically and in summary these three foundations, with attention drawn to the progression of a technology that far exceeds the development of both liberty and brotherhood. The following sections discuss more specifically the rationalism of Greece, the legalism of Rome, and the ethics of Israel.

Greece: Reason

The ancient Greeks were the first true philosophers, lovers of wisdom, and seekers after truth for its own sake. Their rational speculations about the nature of the physical universe and of humankind provided a foundation for what is now termed the scientific method of inquiry. This method (first get the data, then draw tentative conclusions) vastly stimulated the advances of applied science and thus made possible the wonder world of technology of which we are so proud and fearful.

Rome: Law

The Romans were the masterful governmental administrators of ancient times. Having conquered most of the world known to Western people, they imposed a world of peace *(pax Romana)* upon all their subject peoples, as well as over themselves. To make these civic controls successful and local administration easier, the Romans developed a standardized system of law which their legions imposed throughout the empire. This Roman "common law" established the basis for personal freedom among all Roman citizens, wherever they were, because it meant government by the written law, not by the caprice of the ruler. Cicero observed that "As the laws are above magistrates, so are the magistrates above the people; and it may truly be said that the magistrate is speaking law, and the law a silent magistrate."

Out of Roman law developed English common law with its expanding emphasis upon group and individual rights. That English law, transplanted to the New World in the thirteen original American colonies, fostered the spirit of the Declaration of Independence. This, in turn, stimulated the French Declaration of the Rights of Man and, in our own time, the United Nations' Charter and the Universal Declaration of Human Rights. (The Universal Declaration of Human Rights was adopted by the United Nations General Assembly in 1948. It has not yet been ratified by the United States government.) With growing emphasis upon equality as well as liberty, these democratic conceptions have been given recent legal expression in various United States court decisions and in much civil rights legislation.

Israel: Ethics

In the tiny region of Judea thousands of years ago, sensitive men and women became convinced that the deity is One God, a God of justice and of love. From the prophets of Israel, on through Jesus of Nazareth, and into

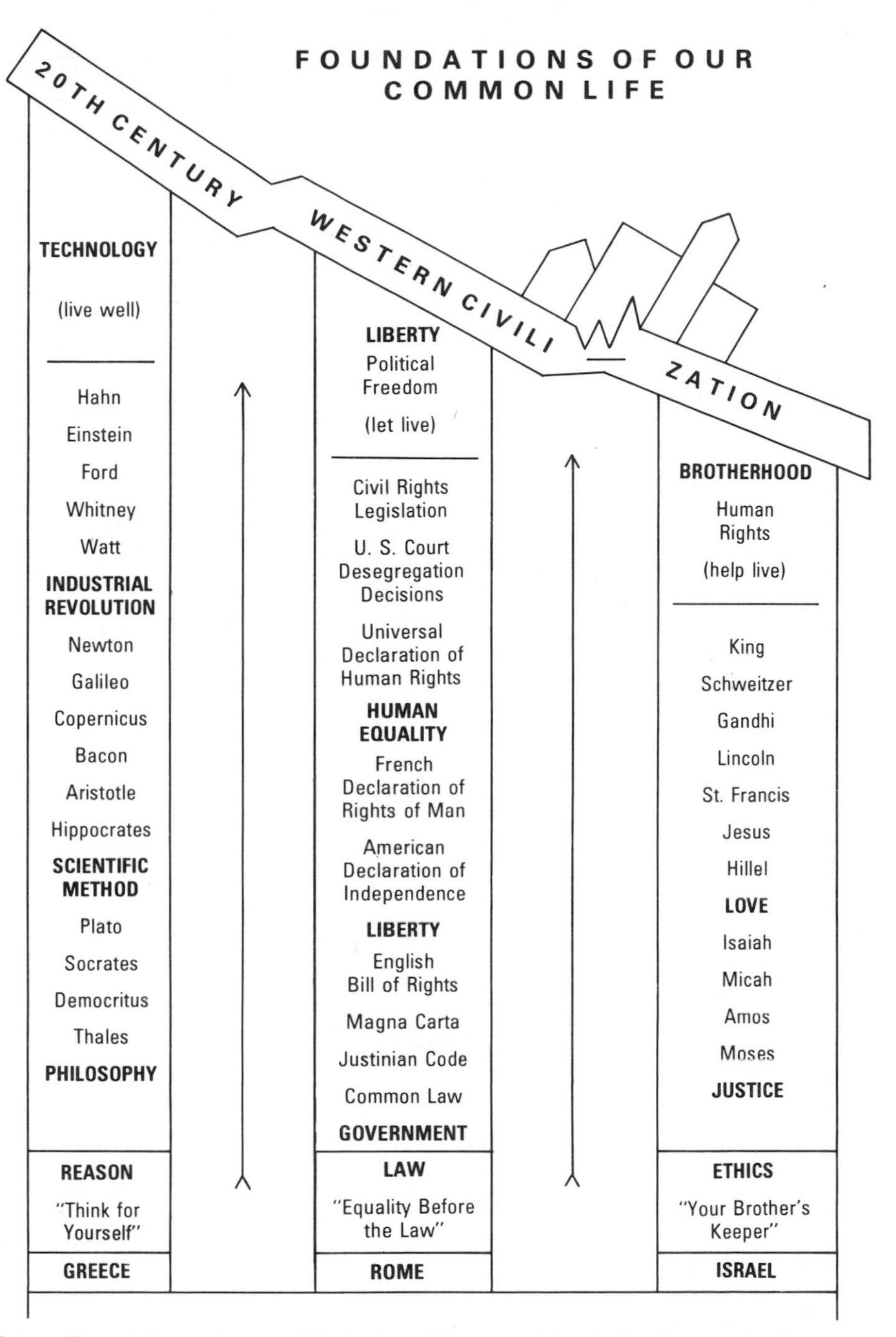

Note: The relative upthrusts of Technology, Liberty, and Brotherhood cannot be drawn to scale. If they were, Technology would appear in miles, Liberty in yards, Brotherhood in inches.

Figure 1

TECHNOLOGY	LIBERTY	BROTHERHOOD
OTTO HAHN — First to split the atom: father of Nuclear Age.	CIVIL RIGHTS LEGISLATION — Outlaws racial, religious ethnic, sex and age discrimination practices.	MARTIN LUTHER KING — Leader in American large-scale, nonviolent resistance to evil racial conditions.
ALBERT EINSTEIN — Relativity theory: basis for research on atom, hence fission.	SUPREME COURT DESEGREGATION DECISION — "In the field of public education the doctrine of 'separate but equal' has no place. Separate educational facilities are inherently unequal . . . "	ALBERT SCHWEITZER — Selfless devotion to physical needs of others, based on idea of "reverence for life."
HENRY FORD — Perfected assembly line methods: mass production in industry.	UNIVERSAL DECLARATION OF HUMAN RIGHTS — "All human beings are born free and equal in dignity and rights. They are endowed with reason and conscience and should act towards one another in a spirit of brotherhood."	MAHATMA GANDHI — Developed technique of mass resistance to unjust social conditions through nonviolent pressures.
ELI WHITNEY — Perfected interchangeable parts: father of mass production.	FRENCH DECLARATION OF THE RIGHTS OF MAN — Declared that basic rights of citizens include Fraternity as well as Liberty and Equality.	ABRAHAM LINCOLN — "Whenever there is conflict between human rights and property rights, human rights must prevail."
JAMES WATT — Invented steam engine: father of Industrial Revolution	AMERICAN DECLARATION OF INDEPENDANCE — "We hold these truths to be self-evident, that all men are created equal, that they are endowed by their Creator with certain unalienable Rights, that among these are Life, Liberty, and the pursuit of Happiness."	ST. FRANCIS — "Lord, make me an instrument of Thy peace."
NEWTON — Formulated law of gravitation; led to concept of orderly, natural-law universe.	ENGLISH BILL OF RIGHTS — Explicit assertion of Parliament's supremacy which marked end of Divine Right of Kings dogma and provided protection for citizens against arbitrary government power.	JESUS CHRIST — "A new commandment I give unto you, that you love one another."
GALILEO — Applied Bacon's method to study of natural world: foundation for modern experimental science.	MAGNA CARTA — Asserted rights of barons against the king: began to limit his absolute power.	HILLEL — "What is hateful to thee, do not do unto thy fellowman; this is the whole Law; the rest is mere commentary."
COPERNICUS — Revolutionized medieval idea of the cosmos.	ENGLISH COMMON LAW — Based indirectly on Roman law; emphasized group and personal rights.	ISAIAH — "They shall beat their swords into plowshares, their spears into pruning hooks, nation shall not lift up hand against nation, neither shall they learn war anymore."
BACON — Father of scientific thinking: get facts, then generalize, test out, etc.	JUSTINIAN CODE — This written Roman law provided basis for government of laws, not of the ruler's caprice.	MICAH — "He hath showed thee, O man, what is good; and what doth the Lord require of thee but to do justly, and to love mercy, and to walk humbly with Thy God?"
ARISTOTLE — First encyclopedist; recorded most known facts in many fields.		AMOS — "Let judgment roll down as waters, and righteousness as a mighty stream."
HIPPOCRATES — Applied scientific approach to study of human body: father of medicine.		MOSES — Recorder of the Ten Commandments.
PLATO — Creator of philosophic system based on universalized ideas of truth, beauty, goodness.		
SOCRATES — Applied cause-and-effect thinking to problems in human relationships.		
DEMOCRITUS — Theorized that all matter is composed of invisible atoms: first atomic thinker.		
THALES — First philosopher: explained physical world in terms of one universal substance.		
REASON	**LAW**	**ETHICS**

FOUNDATIONS OF OUR COMMON LIFE

Figure 2

the lives of modern saints of humanity, the strong belief has flowered that the fatherhood of God requires the brotherhood of man. Through the centuries the Western social conscience has been challenged, aroused, and sometimes swept into ethical action by prophetic religion at its highest and best. This essential Judeo-Christian tradition is indeed basic to our whole historic value system. One of its central expectations is that justice in human relationships always equals, in religious importance, the love of God itself.

Some may object that this portrayal of Western ethical sources is too narrow; that others also should be listed — the Socratic dialogues, Buddhism, Islam, Voltarian rationalism, the Kantian Imperative and the like. Of course, Greek philosophic concern with ethics, especially Plato's thinking, played a part; Platonism became an integral aspect of later Christian theology. Cato, Seneca, and other Roman thinkers also left their imprints upon Western conscience. But Buddhism had been largely unknown in the West until this generation, and even now only a tiny proportion of Americans are aware of its variations and tenets. The Islamic Brotherhood ideal was and is strictly confined to Muslim believers; it has not been universalized as has the Judeo-Christian concept of brotherhood among all peoples. The essential Western ethical vision and hope so widely accepted as an ideal, so generally ignored in living, is in its origin and development basically an Israeli contribution to Western civilization.

SOCIAL AND EDUCATIONAL LAG

Oversimplified as this historical sketch has been, it still may provide a helpful perspective for our education thinking today by putting into sharp and demanding contrast the development, interrelationships and central imperative of human living on our planet in the decades ahead. The sources of Western civilization and American society can be summarized like this:

GREEK REASON produced the scientific method, which developed technology, and brought us into the modern age. Science gives us the technical methods required to *live well* in the material sense of creature comforts and some physical security. So: *Technology we revere.*

ROMAN LAW became the basis of English common law; hence of American jurisprudence with its deep concern for *Liberty* and personal freedom. Liberty means to live and *let live* without oppression of any kind and for all to share in making the decisions which control their lives. And: *Liberty we prize,* at least in theory.

ISRAELI ETHICS gave us our moral law through the Judeo-Christian concern for ethical human relationships based on justice, motivated by love, and expressed in *Brotherhood.* Brotherhood is more than democracy because its concern is to *help others live* more abundant lives in terms of human dignity and mutual respect. But: *Brotherhood we ignore in group relations,* even as we acclaim it as our ideal.

Where, then, are we? We are at a point in history when we simply dare not ignore any longer the basic and perhaps fatal weakness of the world today: the tremendous advance of technology over liberty, and the frightful lag of brotherhood behind both. This is the silent revolution that threatens humankind:

The lag of world organization behind world technology;
The lag of economic distribution behind industrial productivity;
The lag of religion behind ethics;
The lag of education behind life needs.

"We stand with our mechanical foot in an airplane and our social foot in an oxcart," mused Harry Elmer Barnes a generation ago, "and the stretch is becoming painful, not to say dangerous." "This world has achieved brilliance without wisdom," observed five-star General Omar Bradley, "power without conscience. Ours is a world of nuclear giants and ethical infants." Albert Einstein earlier had warned that "The splitting of the atom has changed everything except our modes of thinking, and thus we drift toward unparalleled catastrophe." The World Council of Churches, meeting in Kenya late in 1975, said that the world is on a "catastrophic course leading to mass starvation, global depletion of resources and global environmental deterioration." The Council called for a "radical transformation of civilization."

The stunning question "Can we survive?" was widely publicized in the first major observance in our nation's bicentennial celebration, the EXPO '74 world's fair held in Spokane, Washington. Some of EXPO's striking exhibits forthrightly stated the central issue:

The Earth Does Not Belong to Man; Man Belongs to the Earth.

All over the world people are beginning to realize the significance of the massive accelerating scale of human activity and are beginning to ask: Where are we? Are we in control? How long can it continue like this? 10, 50, 100 years? Has our cleverness outpaced our wisdom?

Man destroys his environment to live. He must now restore it to survive.

Clearly the choice is ours to make. We can choose the kind of world we want to have — ugliness, destruction, waste, lifelessness against beauty, life and natural splendor. It is one of the most clear-cut choices we will ever be given to make. . . . . The sad thing is that the choice we make will be the choice all people will have to live with for all time on this planet.

TRENDS AND PORTENTS

How, then, shall we view the challenge of tumultuous change in our times? Four fundamental factors in modern society together make up this challenge: 1) in our scientific achievements we have entered the nuclear space age; 2) in our intergroup human relationships we are virtually barbarians; 3) democracy is now on trial for its life; and 4) futuristic social planning is our imperative new frontier. Considered separately, these are the great social-civic trends of this century. Together, they force us to face frankly the central moral dilemma and political problem of civilization today: how to learn to use our stupendous technology and our basic social institutions to enhance and not to degrade human life on this planet.

Scientific Achievements

The story is told that Adam and Eve, facing eviction from the Garden of Eden, were talking about the unknown tomorrow. Having enjoyed quiet contentment in familiar and well-ordered surroundings, they were now to be thrust rudely out into a new and terrifying kind of world. "My dear," said Eve to Adam, "we might just as well face the fact. This is the end of an era."

How right she was! They had to leave behind the old, established value system and life styles and stumble forward into a drastically different and far more difficult kind of life. They did not like the prospect, but they had to accept it. For one era *had* ended, and another begun.

So it is today. In truth, our generation stands on the very threshold of a whole new age. When the scientists working under the grandstand at the University of Chicago achieved atomic fission in 1942, they were learning how to rip apart the very building blocks of the universe. That unleashing of incredible primeval power in atomic fission and later in nuclear fusion is as momentous for the future of the human race as was the discovery of fire by primitive man, milleniums ago.

Since 1957, well over three thousand manufactured earth satellites have been circling the planet through outer space. Twelve men have walked on the moon and returned to share their experiences. We confidently expect that in the next decade or two the interplanetary space ships of yesterday's science fiction will become tomorrow's headlines. In November 1974, an ambitious attempt was made to communicate with another civilization in the universe. A powerful, coded radio signal was beamed to a global cluster of 300 thousand stars some 24 thousand light years away on the edge of the Milky Way galaxy. The signals sent information about how we count, the chemistry of life, and our genetic material. In 48 thousand years a reply may be received![5]

As Charles Kettering once observed, in the field of technology there is nothing man can conceive that he cannot achieve sooner or later, and generally sooner than expected. Science and technology rush ever onward and are interactive throughout the world. In these fields we are virtually Supermen

— planetary today, interstellar tomorrow. Already we are hurtling headlong into the thermonuclear space age — with mushroom clouds and awesome photographs of the earth in space as its first symbols.

Human Relations

Everywhere in the world people are engaged in the greatest human revolution in history. Most of them are sharing, in some degree and fashion, the age-old and ever new dreams of overcoming hunger and disease, of conquering poverty and ignorance, of finding dignity and status as individual human beings. That is the real meaning of this century's political upheavals in Russia, India, China, Africa; of Israel and the Arab nations; of Ireland torn by religious-nationalistic fears and hate; of racial and class conflicts in many lands and the whole wide struggle over apartheid and desegregation. The compelling crux of these desperate strivings in every field and area is sharply this: without the spirit and ethic of democracy and brotherhood these emerging upswings of legitimate human aspirations will surely go sour with personal ambition, greed, hate and destruction. British economist Barbara Ward has said it well, albeit in another context: "The only alternatives for man the world over are to move toward equality or to sink into violence and blood."[6]

America's whole history reflects a continuing struggle to gain, protect, and expand human freedom. Was not this value struggle the heart of the Mayflower Compact, Declaration of Independence, Bill of Rights, slave revolts, Emancipation Proclamation, women's suffrage, legal protection of children, early labor movement, civil rights movement, women's liberation, abortion and homosexual freedom conflicts, and the incipient issue of euthanasia? None of us can expect all other people to share our particular idea and pattern of what is right, good, and desirable behavior. This means that each of us must learn to live with interpersonal differences, however strange they may seem to us, and to do so in mutual respect and harmony. This requires calm readiness to give all persons the same chance for food, health, jobs, schooling, housing, recreation and all other aspects of group living that we want for ourselves — within our nation now, and soon on a world basis. Is it not true that doing so is genuine democracy, ethical religion, scientific sense, and sheer self-preservation?

We point to the Berlin Wall with indignation, while blindly ignoring the high walls of prejudice, discrimination and segregation which we still maintain to degrade and separate people from people throughout our nation and the world. How typically we place hand on heart before our flag and solemnly pledge "liberty and justice for all" and in the next moment clench that hand into a threatening fist and growl that never shall *they* secure equal status with *us*!

Is it not transparently clear that in terms of our intergroup human relationships we are often barbarians in modern dress?

Democracy on Trial

As commonly defined, democracy means a form of government in which the supreme political power is vested in the people and is exercised by them directly or by their freely elected representatives. But, in a larger and increasingly symbolic sense, democracy is more than a form of government or a technique for selecting political representatives. It goes far beyond any particular pattern of social living. For democracy is above all else a dynamic common faith in the ability of enlightened people to manage their collective affairs with intelligence, justice, and compassion. Surely the hallmarks of modern democracy must include:

A strong belief that the human mind can be trusted if it is free;
Calm confidence in the methods of cooperative group effort;
Active respect for the human worth and dignity of every individual person regardless of race, religion or lack of it, social status, sexual orientation, ethnic background, or nationality.

Ours is not a middle-class, suburban, white-collar world. It certainly is not a white world. Neither is it a Judeo-Christian world. On this planet now live some four billion human beings. If we think of our big earth as a village with a population of one thousand people, we shall find that in it there are 140 North and South Americans (60 representing the United States); 210 Europeans; 86 Africans; 565 Asians. There are 300 white people and 700 nonwhite people. Of the thousand, 300 are called Christians. Half of the total income of the village comes to the 60 people in the United States. Almost all the affluent part of the village is composed of Christians from Europe and North America. Over 700 of the one thousand villagers are unable to read. Over 500 suffer from malnutrition. Over 800 live in what we call substandard housing. No more than 10 have a university education.

On this day next year there will be some 68 million more living beings on the earth than there are now. Of the nearly 100 thousand babies born every day, four out of five are nonwhite. By the year 2000 (only two decades away!) the world population will likely number over six billion. And most of those people will live in Asia, Africa, Russia and South America.

The varied revolutions now shaking world societies are among the most momentous of modern times. These upheavals — whether in Asia, the Middle East, Africa or elsewhere — are not only political and economic in character. They are also philosophic at heart and as deeply concerned with intergroup value concepts as they are with technology and social power. Their fanatical nationalism and often avowed racism and religionism must not blind us to that truth. Much of the popular support for the dictators of our times is callously grounded upon a psychological foundation of such great moral ideas as the dignity of man and the imperatives of democracy.

It is beside the point to argue that dictatorial leaders are unscrupulous exploiters of their own people. No doubt that has been the case in a number of countries, West and East, and is true in some Third World nations now. The really significant fact is that their basic appeal to public opinion and popular support is grounded in the dynamic moral belief that every person, regardless of race, color, creed, sex or age ought to be able to live in dignity and enjoy equal opportunity to make the most of his or her own talents. This deeply ethical conviction, let us not forget, is central in several world religions, including Judaism and Christianity, and is the very heart of the democratic ideal.

Despite efforts toward détente with Russia and China, the free world is still in conflict with ruthless antagonists, and the dimensions of that free world have narrowed markedly during the past quarter century. Daniel Moynihan, former U.S. Ambassador to the United Nations, recently told an Oregon Business Council that only about two-dozen democracies and two-dozen free enterprise countries remain. "'Democracies are becoming a recessive form of government, like monarchies used to be — something the world is moving from, rather than to,' he said. 'We've taken enough punishment lately to wake ourselves up and realize that we may be in trouble,' Moynihan added."[7]

The conflict increases. Antagonists now include the Third World nations of Africa, Asia, South America and the Middle East as well as the major communist powers. It is a conflict not for territory, resources and material goods alone, but also for the minds and hearts and loyalties of men and women around the globe. And it is a conflict we may well lose, whether or not H-bombs ever fall, unless we actually demonstrate our willingness to live, in national policy and daily practice, the glorious words about democracy we so glibly chant as patriotic ritual. For democracy, if it is to mean very much in our times, must produce the kind of society that is not only safe for cultural and ideological differences, but which also works strenuously, even self-sacrificingly, to develop a just and peaceful multicultural civilization world-wide.

New Frontier

Can we accept the premise that a dangerous gulf exists between our society's technology and brotherhood? Do we agree that a democratic civilization must be culturally pluralist in character? Shall we recognize that democracy, as a way of living together, is literally on trial for its continued life? If so, we can then conclude that in self-defense if nothing more we must insistently increase *effective long-range human planning* as our new frontier in civilization and in education.

We talk these days about outer space, but what about the far more important inner space: the space within the heart and between the ears? Every individual needs to give consideration to the following problems:

Continued air, water, and land pollution of the planet;
Rapid depletion of irreplaceable natural resources;
Population controls in this age of increasing malnutrition;
Polarization between rich and poor, within nations and between them;
Unlimited national sovereignties in the nuclear age;
Maintenance of myths and superstitions regarding racism and sexism;
Continued religious hate within and between nations;
Commercialization of culture for private profit.

Every one of these issues is a critical imperative! With these conditions in mind, anthropologist Margaret Mead spoke to a graduating college class about youth's obligations for the future. She warned them and all youth today:

> . . . I think what's going to have to be done in the next three or four years is for everyone, but especially for the students who are just entering the world, to reevaluate the whole position in this country that we're facing in regard to what we do for money and what money will buy and what money won't buy. . . .
>
> What we're going to have to do is to change the patterns of consumption in this country and in the rest of the world. The same thing is true of energy. Money, this year, can buy for you, at present, all the gas you want, and you can drive as wastefully as ever. This will not be true in the future, and we're not going to have enough energy, and we're going to have to think in terms of energy units instead of in terms of money. . . .
>
> . . . We're going to have to learn that the answers we thought would save the world — at the end of World War II we thought we just had to spread our technology all over the world; everybody would have plenty to eat and lovely skyscrapers and schools just like ours and the whole world would be saved — and we've discovered it doesn't work like that and that if we tried to spread our technology over the whole world we'd simply devastate the world. We'd cut down every tree, we'd use up every single resource and we'd leave a desert.
>
> And so we have to learn something new, and it's going to be rough. But you are the ones that have to ask the questions, you are the ones that have to come in with fresh eyes, most of you haven't tried to live with total responsibility in this world and so you're going to have to have a chance to look at the situation fresh while the older people in it are doing our best to readjust our sights, to reassess the hopes that we had, to realize that we have to change the way in which we are building life up, change it very radically and very responsibly and that it's possible.[8]

The World Future Society held its second general assembly in Washington, D.C. in June 1975. More than two thousand scholar-members came to pool their ideas about present trends and about what to expect in the years ahead if these trends continue as now indicated. Among their conclusions which attracted much support were these:

> Effective leadership will be hard to find in the next quarter century, because today's political institutions can't respond quickly enough to head off rapidly escalating problems. The world, scholars feel, is destined to "lurch from crisis to crisis" until political systems can deal with dangerous trends before they get out of control.
>
> The world has entered a "communications era" dominated by television, the computer and other electronic technologies. The sheer weight of high-speed communications during the next two decades can produce the most informed and aware generation in history — or reduce the globe to a second "tower of Babel," collecting and transmitting much information but offering little comprehension of what it all means.
>
> The core issue facing modern man is to strike a balance between the world's teeming population and the earth's shrinking resources, and the time remaining to find a way to resolve this question is critically short.
>
> Thus, global crises that may include nuclear terrorism, oil wars, widespread famine and political revolution are almost certain to occur before the end of the century.[9]

Commenting on these sobering conclusions, *U. S. News & World Report* noted that "What this all means is that long-term planning over many aspects of life — work roles, health care, personal consumption, family size, mobility from urban to rural areas — is inevitable. But experts hope that it can be done through a form of 'anticipatory democracy' in which citizens at state and community levels try to forecast problems and set in motion efforts to resolve them before they occur."

Are these conclusions devastating? They had better be so, for they represent some of the imperatives confronting world society today. What can we do about them? Who is responsible for attempts at correcting them? Do education institutions have a responsibility to address these imperatives? Do *all* people and institutions have a responsibility to work toward solving these critical problems? Should the curricula of our education institutions be evaluated to determine how well they address themselves to the *life concerns* of all people on this earth?

SPACESHIP EARTH

Former U. S. Ambassador to the United Nations, Adlai Stevenson, II dramatized our central educational challenge in his last public speech, given in Geneva, Switzerland, just before his death in 1965:

> We travel together, passengers on a little space ship, dependent on its vulnerable reserves of air and soil; all committed for our safety to its security and peace; preserved from annihilation only by the care, the work, and I will say the love we give our fragile craft. We cannot maintain it half fortunate, half miserable; half confident, half despairing; half slave to the ancient enemies of man, half free in this day. No craft, no crew can travel safely with such vast contradictions.

On this little Spaceship Earth we urgently require a new and universal approach to formal education. The curricula of our institutions should become functional plans for sequential, cumulative and realistic individual and group learning experiences based on the facts that there is only one species of mankind on our planet and that this is indeed an endangered species. None of the devastating problems endangering human life today — war, pollution, poverty, population — can be solved except on a global basis. Norman Cousins, editor of the *Saturday Review-World,* exposed the heart and depth of the international education problem we must confront when he wrote:

> The prime failure of modern society is that it has neither the philosophy nor the institutions to deal with crimes against humanity itself. Public fear and indignation are aroused by palpable things — a woman assaulted in a doorway, the hijacking of a plane, the terroristic bombing of a school bus, Watergates. But the conversion of masses of men into killers, the disfiguration of human values on a mammoth scale by governments themselves, the diversion of natural resources and human energies into the means of senseless total destruction, the assault on the conditions of life, the puncturing of the ozone layer — these are towering crimes. The failure to see them as such is a danger in itself.
>
> The governments persist in their policies despite the fact that no nation can wage nuclear war against another without also going to war against the human race. Even the preparation for such a conflict is tantamount to an act of war against the species. Yet there is no institution in this world that can pull the nations back from the brink, that can define crimes against humanity and act against criminals, that is capable of making and carrying out moral judgments, or that can uphold the rights of the next generation.[10]

Somehow people must learn to know and to feel that, although they are members of this or that sex, nation, race, religion, or culture, they are primarily all members of one human race, totally dependent on the same earth life-support system. Somehow they must all come to realize with astronaut Frank Borman that "We are one hunk of ground, water, air, clouds, floating around in space. From out there it really is 'one world.' "

A tumultuous world? Unquestionably! Even so, a great world civilization is still possible. We may trust that historian Arnold Toynbee was right when he predicted that "the Twentieth Century will be chiefly remembered not as an age of political conflict or technical inventions, but as an age in which human society dared to think of the welfare of the whole human race as a practicable objective."[11]

Elsewhere, Toynbee stated starkly the two alternatives before the world today:

> In the Atomic Age, mankind has to choose between political unification and mass suicide . . . [yet] the Western society has shown itself exceptionally recalcitrant to any movement towards political unification hitherto, and this Western peculiarity is a handicap to present-day mankind as a whole, since, in our time, the non-Western majority of the human race is adopting Western manners and customs, Western ideas and ideals, and Western likes and dislikes. However, the fashionable Western liking for political disunity and dislike of political unity is no more than a habit that has found its way into the social and cultural heritage of one section of the human race. It is not a built-in trait of human nature even in the West, and, *a fortiori,* not in the rest of the world, where it is being adopted today in its distinctive Western form. Since habits can be acquired and adopted, they can also be modified and abandoned. We do give up even the most cherished habits if and when it becomes clear that it will be disastrous to persist in them; and the accelerating progress of technology has already made it clear that it will be disastrous now not to give up the habit of political disunity in at least two fields in which the only alternative to a catastrophe lies in common action on a world-wide scale. We are going to have to establish one world-authority to control atomic energy and another to administer the production and distribution of food. These unwelcome steps towards the political unification of the world are being forced upon us by the technological revolution that we ourselves have engineered. . . . It therefore seems probable that, as the lesser evil, we shall submit to at least the minimum of world-government that we see to be immediately necessary for salvation, though we shall submit to this grumbling and growling, and shall hold back till the eleventh hour.[12]

Purely political solutions, however imperative, are not going to save our present industrial civilization, asserts Alvin Toffler in his *Eco-Spasm Report:*

> What we are seeing (today) is the general crisis of industrialism — a crisis that transcends the differences between capitalism and Soviet-style communism, a crisis that is simultaneously tearing up our energy base, our value systems, our sense of space and time, our epistemology as well as our economy. What is happening, no more, no less, is the breakdown of industrial civilization on the planet and the first fragmentary appearance of a wholly new and drastically different social order: a super-industrial

civilization that will be technological, but no longer industrial.[13]

Gloomy as that prospect may appear, concludes Toffler, it is not entirely disastrous.

> One might also look upon the coming years of trauma as the long-needed opportunity to set some old problems straight — to overhaul some of our creaking, undemocratic political institutions; to humanize technology; to think our way through a fresh set of both personal and political priorities. To re-examine the blind faith we have in the processes of economic integration. To think not merely about minimum living standards but perhaps about maximum ones; to move, in short, toward some concept of enoughness so that energies, imagination, and passion can begin to flow into dimensions of growth long ignored by us. To re-evaluate the notions of individualism and collectivism, seeing them not as mutually exclusive Aristotelian opposites, but as necessary to one another. To invent new institutions, family styles, fusions of work and meaning. In short, to undertake an awesome but exhilarating task that few generations in human history have ever faced: the design of a new civilization.[14]

No blueprints for such a new and truly humane society are presently available, but the *goal-setting basic values* upon which it must be built were spelled out in the Universal Declaration of Human Rights. That declaration, a "Magna Carta for the earth," was unanimously adopted by the Assembly of the United Nations in 1948. Its essence, as sketched by Richard E. Gilbert in *Ethics for Everybody,* a bicentennial project of The Interchurch Center, is both exciting and demanding of the highest statesmanship:

1. Every person is a somebody — unique, independent, entitled to life and security.
2. Every person is equal before the law — no discrimination permitted.
3. Every person is a world citizen — entitled to move freely across frontiers.
4. Every person is a free citizen — free to marry, own property and express opinions.
5. Every person is a political citizen — entitled to a government based on the people's will.
6. Every person is a money-maker — entitled to social, cultural and economic security.
7. Every person is a learner — with free access to education.
8. Every person is a *respecter* of the rights of others — we *are* our brother's keepers.

Idealistic? Yes. Visionary? Certainly. Practical? The only way to go! For without vision the people perish.

EDUCATION AND CIVILIZATION

President Lawrence A. Cremin of Teachers College, Columbia University, voices the following concerns and puts them squarely before educators in immediate terms. He says that:

> To talk about the sciences and arts of education without talking about the values, aspirations, and ideals of the civilization that education is intended to bring into being, is to talk about a monstrosity. The only way we can conceive a great education is to conceive a great civilization. Along with the sciences and arts of education, we must cultivate . . . an informed and imaginative vision of what education might mean in a truly humane society — a democratic society, committed to the equality of all human beings and the worth of their individual lives; a free society, where each and every individual is afforded a rich and varied opportunity to develop his or her potential to the fullest; a transnational society that conceives of its public life as extending, not merely to all Americans, but to every man, woman and child on earth.[15]

If such a democratic, transnational society is ever to emerge, it will have to be *built* by the combined and sustained educational efforts of all institutions committed to the hope of achieving common unity. That means governments, religions, public and private organizations, the mass media, schools, and many others. For, if the twentieth century sequence of social upheavals means anything at all, it must be this: that now, and into the next generation, we must really begin to learn to live well together as One Family of Man. If we cannot, do not, or will not, then civilization as we know and desire it can hardly continue. In our times science and technology have made the whole world into one vast physical neighborhood, yet the neighbors are by no means neighborly. Our world's primary problem is to match liberty and brotherhood with technology — to create in the world neighborhood a humane community wherein men and women of all nations, colors, creeds, culture patterns and value systems can learn to live together in harmony, peace and plenty.

That kind of community-building is not something far off in time or in space; it is not just a glorious ideal; it is now the practical necessity. This nation, and all nations, must somehow find and implement a new and vital moral human purpose: that of building the educational, psychological, economic and political bases for a genuine world community. The whole history of humankind has been one of expanding areas within which the people have felt a "we" sense of kinship and purpose: from family group to tribe, to city-state, to nation, and to aggregates of nations. The final stage is now our planetary imperative to develop a profound and mutual feeling of common unity, of *community,* among peoples within nations and between peoples of all nations.

Human community, a profound and general sense of *common unity,* is the crucial essence of any enduring free society, small or large. Without that fundamental public sense of shared values, of community aspirations, no democratic framework is likely to survive for even another generation. If we are to continue as a free and culturally pluralistic people, we must immediately seek substantial ways to build up the imperative psychological basis for genuine community development in family groups, neighborhoods, urban areas, geographic regions, the nation, and in the larger world of human beings everywhere.

Myriads of youthful Americans deeply feel this parched-ground hunger for genuine community to replace the constrictive, dehumanizing, and frustrating life patterns still dominant. Many not so young share that longing also. Among them is Harold Taylor, former president of Sarah Lawrence College and world-minded international educator. He is realistic about the present world and optimistic for its future. In his view:

> . . . the principal fact of the modern world is not its massive unrest, although that is its most visible charcteristic, but its growing and necessary unity — the inter-penetration of all lives by every other, the coming-together of peoples, cultures, and societies to accomplish common purposes. There exists beneath the surface of the visible world society an inner community of persons — peasants, teachers, doctors, scientists, students, lovers, composers and others, linked together intuitively by common concerns and interests, friendly to the needs of the human race and reaching out to each other across the divisions of the world and its governments. . . .
>
> The teacher is at the center of this new community. So is the student. They share, in whatever country they live and under whatever political system, a common interest in the work of the mind and the use of intelligence to advance learning for human benefit. In the United States a new generation of students has created a national community among themselves, with national and international interests, of which the problems of peace and war, human rights, the politics of change and the reform of education are central. They see problems in world society in the same light as they see their own.[16]

In these tumultuous times what can we do — we citizens, teachers, students, school administrators and board members, community leaders in many fields — what can we *do* to design and develop quality education for the 1980s and beyond? How shall we see our primary responsibility in the rushing race between realistic education and social catastrophe? What can we *do* that is genuinely constructive rather than superficially busy? How can we together create a new nd effective educational process and curricular program that will help people learn to live well together as unique individuals still? Can we develop education for social transformation within a schizoid culture? How can we use the education institutions we already have by greatly improving their purposes, processes and programs? Is not this our job for the new age?

These are indeed searching queries, for they involve one's whole philosophy of society as well as varied conceptions of education. They are questions each educator, student and citizen must answer to his or her own satisfaction, in terms of personal diagnosis of social trends and their implications for living today and tomorrow. With the early twentieth century historian H. G. Wells we had better realize and act now upon the profound perception that "Human history becomes more and more a race between education and catastrophe."

The National Education Association in 1975 adopted the following resolution pertaining to education:

A DECLARATION OF INTERDEPENDENCE:
EDUCATION FOR A GLOBAL COMMUNITY

We hold these truths to be self-evident:

THAT 200 years after declaring our independence, the American people are entering a new era.

THAT today we must acknowledge the interdependence of all people.

THAT education can be a vehicle through which peace and the principles of the American Revolution — life, liberty, and the pursuit of happiness — may be the guidelines for human relationship on our planet.

THAT educators around the world are in a unique position to help bring about a harmoniously interdependent global community based on the principles of peace and justice.

THAT toward this end the National Education Association is pursuing a series of programs to prepare for major reform in education.

How well equipped are our conventional schools and colleges to assist in this imperative process of essential self-and-social education? *That* is the concern of the next chapter.

2. SCHOOLS IN CRISIS

Because adults take the schools so much for granted, they fail to appreciate what grim, joyless places most American schools are, how oppressive and petty are the rules by which they are governed, how intellectually sterile and aesthetically barren their atmosphere, what an appalling lack of civility obtains on the part of the teachers and principals, what contempt they unconsciously display for children as children. . . .

What is mostly wrong with the public schools is due not to venality or indifference or stupidity, but to mindlessness. . . . By and large, teachers, principals, and superintendents are decent, intelligent, and caring people who try to do their best by their lights. If they make a botch of it, and an uncomfortably large number do, it is because it simply never occurs to more than a handful to ask why *they are doing what they are doing — to think seriously or deeply about the purpose or consequences of education. . . .*

What is education for? What kind of human beings and what kind of society do we want to produce? What methods of instruction and classroom organization, as well as what subject matter, do we need to produce these results? What knowledge is of most worth?

— Charles E. Silberman, *Crisis in the Classroom*

On the school scene today the name of the game is Trouble. In many communities, large and small, 3-D trouble prevails: Dollar trouble, Dropout trouble, and Disbelief trouble. Despite extensive and expensive federal aid, more than one-half of all school tax and bond elections fail every year, some of them repeatedly. Each year, about a million boys and girls leave high school before graduating. Behind them are millions more who are psychological dropouts; their bodies are still in school, but they are indifferent to education, alienated from the school program, even hostile to the intellectual life. Parents ask, "What's the matter with the schools these days? They don't teach kids much, and they can't even keep them in line." Teachers say, "We try so hard; every approach we know; but many just don't care. They don't want to learn." Students lament, "Why does the school keep putting us down? Why doesn't it teach us about real problems? Most of that stuff they talk about doesn't mean anything, really. What good is all that to us?" Many people are concerned, saying, "We believe in education. It's important and it's necessary to get ahead. But schools nowadays aren't doing their job as they used to do. What *is* the matter with them?"

Education, a mainstay of the American Dream since the nation's founding, is very much in crisis.

SOBERING STUDIES

Why? What is wrong? What is causing these troubles? How effective are the schools, really? To answer such questions, comprehensive school system surveys have been conducted over the years, and friendly critics as well as others have made individual studies. Partial summaries of a few more significant surveys and studies reveal remarkable similarities in their general findings and conclusions. Beginning with two intensive analyses of New York State schools made thirty-three years apart, the contrasts prove interesting.

> 1938 — The New York Board of Regents inquired into the character and cost of public school education. The conclusion reached was that "the schools as a whole have not been able to keep up with the growing world in which we live. . . . The school system is now turning out a great number of youth each year, with and without diplomas, who are not adequately educated, who are not prepared to play a helpful part in the life of this State. Many are not ready to become citizens and to take a useful part in community and family life. Many are not ready to go to work. . . . Many are not ready for advanced or professional education, not ready to pursue their own intellectual or technical development. . . . There is but one conclusion: our education system is not all we want it to be; it is not fully doing the task we have assigned it."[1]

> 1972 — The New York State Commission on the Quality, Cost and Financing of Elementary and Secondary Education was appointed late in 1969 by joint action of Governor Rockefeller and the Board of Regents of the State of New York. Its mission was to produce the most comprehensive report ever authorized by a single state. After two years of intensive study the Commission stated that "A review of such indicators as truancy and dropout rates and the high degree of youth unemployment shows us that too many students are leaving school without mastering the basic academic skills, with no interest in continuing their education and, too frequently, with inadequate preparation for work. For many students who plan to continue their education, the last two years of high school are unproductive and repetitious.[2]

A third of a century elapsed between these two state-wide surveys of public schools! Was there no genuine advance in all that time? Like Alice in Wonderland, were the schools only running hard so as not fall backward?

The National Commission on the Reform of Secondary Education issued in 1973 its report on conditions in America's high schools. This was the first comprehensive study taken since 1918 when a National Education Association Commission formulated the famous "Seven Cardinal Principles" as a guide for redesigning high school goals and, by implication, the curriculum. The recent Commission included students and legislators as well as educators. Its basic conclusions were that high schools generally are in a "beleaguered condition" and that "Our large city school systems are on the verge of complete collapse."[3] The Commission made numerous recommendations for reform, especially in the problem areas of citizen involvement, programs of citizenship education, and the management of alternative schools and programs.

In 1974 a National Panel on High Schools and Adolescent Education turned a sweeping searchlight on youth education. The Panel was chaired by John Henry Martin, a former superintendent of schools. It included widely known scholars, students, and eminent representatives of several fields. The Panel's report to the United States Office of Education was concisely summarized by James Cass, Education Editor of *Saturday Review/World:*

> In an effort to keep the schools free of partisan politics and the pressures of vested interests, educators have isolated the schools from the community and from the informal but powerful "collateral education" that students receive from television and the other media, from work experience, and from other institutions in the community. Education has come to mean simply what happens in the schools.
>
> The successful absorption of the vast majority of teen-aged adults into the self-contained high school has "decoupled" and alienated the generations, delayed the entry of youth into the real adult world, and deprived them of adult models, other than teachers and parents.
>
> Despite clear evidence that young people today mature physically two years earlier than their grandparents — and the assumption that there is comparable intellectual growth — the schools typically treat them as children. "We baby-sit, at very high cost during the day, the nation's night-time babysitters: we trust our infants to their care but impose childish and costly controls over them."
>
> Two of the basic missions of the comprehensive high school — education for citizenship and vocational training — are manifest failures. The authoritarian and bureaucratic rigidities of the typical school do not provide an environment conducive to training for democratic citizenship. And vocational education characteristically trains young people for jobs that no longer exist instead or for a future in which most individuals are likely to have a variety of occupations.
>
> The panel, therefore, calls for a *shift in emphasis from the comprehensive school to "comprehensive education"* (italics supplied) and argues that

> "the confines of one building [can] no longer contain all the valuable and necessary experience for today's young person." It would decentralize secondary education by moving part of it out into the community and by bringing more of the community back into the school in programs for the joint participation of adolescent and other interested . . . adults in the community.[4]

Numerous recommendations were made by this Panel, especially in the areas of art, vocational and civic education. It called for greatly expanded firsthand experience, including all-age-level participation, on-the-job experience, direct involvement of students in governmental agencies and other activities carried on in the community, but tied to school seminars and classes. The Panel also called for "a gradual shortening of the school day to two to four hours — the time that is actually devoted to instruction in the schools — and for re-emphasizing of the 'basic role of the high school as society's only universal institution for the education of the intellect.' "

In 1975 the four-year Adult Performance Level study of the U.S. Office of Education reported that at least one in five adult Americans lacks the basic educational skills to function competently on the job or in the marketplace, in looking after his health or participating fully in his government and community.

This study sought to discover how well people could cope with such daily problems as making change, understanding an insurance policy, where to apply for Social Security, what skills are required for different jobs, and the like. Five areas of knowledge were measured: Consumer economics, occupational information, government and law, health, and community resources. Also tested were four basic skills: Reading, problem solving, computation and writing. Among the findings were these:

> 20% of those surveyed did not know the meaning of the sign "We are an Equal Opportunity Employer."
>
> 14% could not properly write a bank check.
>
> 27% were unaware that normal body temperature is 98.6 F.
>
> 34% believed that police have the right to detain a suspect for as long as a week without bringing charges.

The study concluded:

> As long as "literacy" is conceived to be nothing more than the ability to read and write one's name, or to score at some low grade level on a standardized test developed for children, then the United States does not have a significant problem. On the other hand, if the concern is with the adult who does not possess those skills and knowledge which are requisite to adult competence, then the results of (our) research suggest that there is, indeed, a widespread discrepancy in our adult population between what is required of them and what they achieve. *

**The Oregonian*, October 30, 1975.

Former U.S. Commissioner of Education Terrel H. Bell described the findings as "rather startling," and said they "call for some major rethinking of education on several levels." *

In 1975 the Kettering Foundation's Task Force '74 reported the results of its follow-up study of the National Commission on the Reform of Secondary Education's conclusions. This Task Force, like the earlier group, was composed of state legislators, teachers, school administrators, academic associations and others. Its members traveled widely, visited schools, utilized many different consultants and studied volumes of materials. Focusing their investigations upon problems of citizen involvement, citizenship education and alternative school programs, they concluded that, "unless many of the problems highlighted . . . receive high priority on our nation's work list, the vitality of our free public education system will be in jeopardy. Though its members are not alarmists, the Task Force concluded that the democratic foundations of our country will be threatened if solutions to these problems are not found."

The Task Force further concluded that within the lifetime of people still active:

Mass communication, especially television, has destroyed the vitality of local and regional cultures, placing on the school greater burdens of acculturation to a vague, undefinable national ethic;

The automobile and the national highway network have accentuated the rootlessness of an already restless society;

Technology has changed people's perceptions of their relationship to their own work and increasingly separated the home from the job;

Affluence has made children, and especially adolescents, consumers on a grand scale and thus subject as individuals to all the pressures of the consumer society;

Family ties have weakened everywhere; and the home nexus from which students come — and to which they must return every evening — has become increasingly unstable and insecure;

The institution of the high school is not insulated from these changes in the larger society.[5]

The Task Force believed that fundamental educational reform at the high school level is imperative and that such reform must be based upon principles which revolve around the following proposals:

Citizens and parents must become more involved in the activities of high schools;

Students must be informed of their rights and assured that such rights will be supported by due process procedures;

Educating for responsibility must become a primary function of the school itself;

*Quoted in *Time,* November 10, 1975.

> Alternative programs to the traditional high school must be tested and established.[6]

One Task Force conclusion given italicized emphasis in the report and one that is especially relevant to the thesis of this book was that *"The challenge to the schools is to no longer attempt to avoid the clash of ideas and value systems which resound in society but to meet them head on through curricular revision."*[7]

Many individual critics have assessed school quality in recent years. One is Robert Finch, former Secretary of Health, Education and Welfare, who lamented that "All too often we are stuffing the heads of the young with the products of earlier innovation rather than teaching them how to innovate. We treat their minds as storehouses to be filled rather than as instruments to be used."[8]

Another outspoken critic of traditional schools is John Bremer, former director of the Parkway ("School Without Walls") Program in the Philadelphia School District. He concluded that:

> Our curriculum belongs, essentially, to the last century. First of all, the choice of subjects to be studied and the parts of those subjects to be emphasized or omitted reflect the social values and problems of the age in which they were chosen — which are not, for the most part, our contemporary values and problems. . . . Large areas suitable for genuine inquiry are omitted altogether. Where are the structure of society and the means of social control studied? Where do we study the ways of making money? Where do we study economic organization in our society? Where do we study the law? If these things are not studied, neither are such areas as human physical and mental disease and human sexual life, and neither are such matters as religion and work. All the most important and personal areas, in which ignorance and obscurantism can do the greatest harm, we omit.[9]

John Holt, author of several best-selling books on children and education, says that:

> Schools act as a jail — they are frankly custodial institutions. In no other American institution — only in prison, would you find the limitations on inherent freedoms of speech and movements one finds in the school system. Not even the most maximum security prisons set aside six hours a day when the inmates are not allowed to talk or move around freely — only in the schools do we make children sit quietly at a desk for six hours a day.[10]

In *Future Shock* Alvin Toffler documented what has happened to the whole societal context of education — a fantastic acceleration in the rate of social change itself. He pointed out that this roaring current of change "has become so powerful today that it overturns institutions, shifts our values and shrivels our roots." He might have added that it tends to shrivel our professional perspective and our innovative imagination also. In a later writing he challenges the whole traditional academic curriculum as being obsolete and largely irrelevant because its orientation is backward to the past, not forward to the future. Its procedures imprison the students rather than liberate them. Its usual academic contents are minutae, instead of the great issues and value conflicts to be recognized and faced in the process of building a better future.[11]

So disillusioned with the schools is Ivan Illich that he has proposed to abolish schools altogether as being beyond reform possibility. They should be totally replaced, he argued in *De-Schooling Society,* with an informal and noncompulsory network of educative community resources.

All such analyses, studies and surveys drive us to ask with all good will why the conventional schools are as they are? Why is their curriculum orientation still backward, not future-centered? Why do most of the classroom learnings they require of students perpetuate the dead past rather than prepare them for the exciting future? Why are school administrators often bureaucrats instead of genuine educational leaders? And why are so many teachers weary manipulators of dreary subject matter, not eager coordinators and interpreters of life-relevant learning experiences?

Marshall McLuhan once dramatized the backward orientation of most schools and educators, as part of society generally, with his analogy of a person driving a car at a high rate of speed with eyes fixed on the rear-view mirror. Why is this so? Must it always be so? Will the inevitable crash occur? Or is it occurring?

Meanwhile, the fourth graders of our Bicentennial year become the high school graduates of 1984, and this date has for a long time been a symbol of drastic and oppressive change. Should not we ask with much insistence: What positive educational experiences are we going to give them and all other children to help them learn to live personally satisfying and socially constructive lives in the rest of the 1970s, the 1980s, the 1990s and on into the first half of the twenty-first century?

ROOTS OF FAILURE

There is no question that conventional schools are failing to prepare people to live creatively, effectively and democratically at this time and place in history. Reasons for that failure are multiple, but an underlying cause is certainly the fact that schools are organized and administered primarily for teaching (sometimes janitorial) ease and convenience, rather than learning effectiveness. Also, their curricula are designed generally for above-average, middle-class children destined for higher education; not for the youngsters who are outside that social milieu and prospect, or who, within it still, are reflecting the Establishment's value system and operations.

Briefly discussed below are some additional factors that contribute to conventional school failure. These are lip service goals, passive programs, nonresponsiveness to feedback, inflexible structures, lack of affective education, and irrelevant content. Readers can undoubtedly add much flesh to the bones of these failure roots.

School officials, including teachers, routinely assert, i.e., give lip service to, the validity of the triple function of the school: to preserve the heritage, to prepare individuals, and to improve society. But in administrative and curricular practice, they heavily overweigh the heritage role, cut small and narrowly short the preparation role, and markedly minimize the societal transformation responsibility of the school.

Much of the school day is undeniably passive, designed for listening and viewing, less for reading and discussion, and still less for all-sensory activity. It appears to be programmed least for community learning experiences, except in the case of athletics, dramatics and other extracurricular events, which are *real* and therefore highly motivate students and bring them genuine personal growth outside the classroom, laboratory, and library.

The learner's evaluative and creative reactions to curriculum or to teaching procedures are rarely sought, heard, or respected. The most common complaint made by students at all levels is that "teachers just don't listen to us." Hence, there is an inexcusable nonresponsiveness to the experience feedback of the persons for whom education is designed.

Even if the school has a "track" system, everyone going through the same field of knowledge is put through the same basic, inflexible structure. In contrast with the extracurricular activities, the academic curriculum is highly inflexible and irresponsive to varied individual differences in student abilities, interests and concerns.

The traditional curriculum is almost exclusively dominated by the cognitive (knowledge) goal; the affective (emotional, feeling) areas of students' lives are widely ignored. There appears to be little actual curricular attention to those concerns and worries that seem to bug people the most.

Much of learning required in the academic subject fields is less than meaningful to most young people today. It is prepackaged primarily to produce academic superiority in its particular area as an end in itself, or for academic acceptability later, rather than as a means to more effective personal and social living outside as well as inside the school.

Is it not obvious that American schools must be drastically transformed in philosophy, procedures and programs? Leon Lessinger, former chief of the United States Office of Education's Bureau of Elementary and Secondary Education, has proposed that schools and colleges must now develop a new tradition; they must change from blaming students when they fail, to accepting the reality of the school's own failure with the students. That acceptance, with all of its implications for educational reconstruction, is long overdue.

YOUTH OUTLOOKS

Enrolled in our schools right now is a new generation of youth quite different from those many of us have known in the past. The youth vary greatly in abilities, aspirations, interests and concerns. Many of them, in greater or lesser degree, have become sensitive to what they consider the decadence of adult society and the futility of much of traditional school and college programs. Some of these are the young people who by their attire and life styles often, though not always, visibly reject the value systems and authoritarian patterns of the adult society and its institutions, including schools and formal education. Even more than that, they are insistently asking that their education be made meaningful and significant to their own lives, here and now. Some of them are dedicated to the bold task of transforming our present society into something far better. They are often impatient, sometimes hostile, and occasionally violent in their reactions because persons in power positions appear so blind to the great needs and so slow to get on with the tasks.

In the latter 1960s, many young people took a hard look at part of our culture; that is, at its values, assumptions, preoccupations and activities. Some of them in the counter-culture challenged the whole social scene with angry tongue and pointed finger:

> Look at you, blowing up whole countries for the sake of some crazy ideologies that you don't live up to anyway. Look at you, mindfucking a whole generation of kids into getting a revolving charge account and buying your junk. (Who's a junkie?) Look at you, needing a couple of stiff drinks before you have the balls to talk with another human being. Look at you, making it with your neighbor's wife on the sly just to try and prove that you're really alive. Look at you, hooked on your "cafeteria" pills, and making up dirty names for anybody who isn't in your bag, and screwing up the land and the water and air for profit, and calling this nowhere scene the Great Society! And you're gonna tell us how to live? C'mon, man, you've got to be kidding![12]

Such sardonic rhetoric was often heard on university campuses as the youth revolt developed steam during the United States' involvement in the Southeast Asia civil war. Today, the organized protests of that period are largely gone, but their impact has profoundly influenced our culture. By all accounts, the present generation of youth has in one dimension returned to the dollar, while in another they have become more existential in values, goals and life styles. In varied ways they seek meaningful guidelines for their lives, their work, their relationships, even as they strive for entry and advancement in the conventional marketplace. As one of them whimsically put it, "I just got word that I am approved for a credit card at Sears; thus do the tentacles of Modern Life reach out to hold me in their clammy embrace; and I seek for greater entanglement even as I rail against it."[13]

Many others, however, younger and perhaps less perceptive, are currently in a mood that is more "I want to feel good, succeed professionally, get established and enjoy the good life with my family."[14] A recent *Scholastic* survey reports that nearly half of all young Americans now believe that democracy is alive and well in this country, and that the nation's political system is working rather well. Vietnam and the results of Watergate are seen as proof that the democratic system does work.[15]

Sometimes acquiescent, perhaps more often extreme, youth's social views, their recurring challenge to older citizens and educators, must not be ignored, evaded, or put down. Many of them are demanding to be shown the relevance of academic tradition to the burning issues of a world on the edge of catastrophe. Somehow they have learned the ideals of their brotherhood cultural heritage. They believe in equality, peace, environmentalism, love and humane individualism. They reject the technological and ideological pragmatism which has produced our Western civilization now so dominated by materialism, exploitation, violence and cynicism. They challenge us to develop quality education of a high order but with a new basic orientation, policy and program: that of mutually accountable youths and adults participating in the remaking of our culture. They challenge educators to help everyone, of all ages, interests and backgrounds, to become deeply aware of the vast gulf between our hopes for the future and the prospects for achieving them. They challenge us to help people face courageously and creatively the great human problems of our time: a cruelly crowded earth, mass starvation, environmental poisoning, constant threat of annihilation, and other such devastating concerns. At their best these discontented young people — and some not so young! — challenge us, all together, to *share ethically in the building of a truly humane society of dignity and decency for all;* a civilization in which our vaunted American Pledge of "liberty and justice for all" becomes a living reality for all people.

This sobering, mighty challenge is not new. Two decades ago, as World War II came to its end, the prestigious yearbook of the American Association of School Administrators said it well:

> Western man now lives between two worlds. One world ended over Japan on August 6, 1945. The new world that is to replace it is struggling to be born. The former world was a compromise, between the ideals of the Western culture and an insatiable lust for power and material goods. It was a world of extremes — of great humanitarianism and unparalleled

savagery; of immense wealth and direst poverty; of mighty works and reckless destruction; of high ethics and ruthless competition; of great progress in the arts and sciences and moral decay in human relationships. Its resources of natural power became the playthings of the strong; coal, oil, railroads, ships, and timber their most cherished possessions; science and technology the handmaidens of their enterprise. It was a world kept in delicate and precarious balance by power politics and the art of the diplomat. This world is ended. To the extent the new world is patterned on the old, the end of Western civilization draws nearer.

It is the function of education to help build a new world in which men and nations may live together in justice and security, in unity and peace. Our ideals have been distilled from the dreams of prophets and sages, and the highest aspirations of men through the ages. It is now the function of education to help give them full expression. It is the great function of the schools of America *to establish with all pupils in the transmission of the culture the moral and spiritual values and the fundamental understandings essential to the improvement of the culture, and necessary for the responsible living together of free men in a free society.*[16]

That exciting summons put forth by the American Association of School Administrators — far more imperative now than then — can best be viewed as one among three central responsibilities and hence operative roles of today's schools and colleges. These three basic responsibilities — to preserve the heritage, to prepare the individual, to transform society — are visualized in Figure 3 and discussed in the next section.

IMPERATIVE EDUCATION

A primary purpose of the school is certainly to preserve the best of the human heritage by inculcating in the minds of each new generation some selected aspects of that heritage. Reading, writing, speaking and basic arithmetic are obviously imperative as communicating and learning tools. But beyond these essentials, what bodies of knowledge are important as background for effective and satisfying living in these and future times? On this issue there is much dispute and continued curriculum tinkering.

Equally vital is the goal of preparing individuals to cope with life's processes and problems, both personal and social. Many schools have also accepted this responsibility.

Rarely, however, have schools recognized and accepted in curricular practice a third and also primary role: that is, one of helping transform society by developing generations of citizens who are deeply and disturbingly aware of pressing needs, central issues, varied proposals for better living, resources available, and the obstacles apparent, and who are person-

THE SCHOOL'S RESPONSIBILITIES

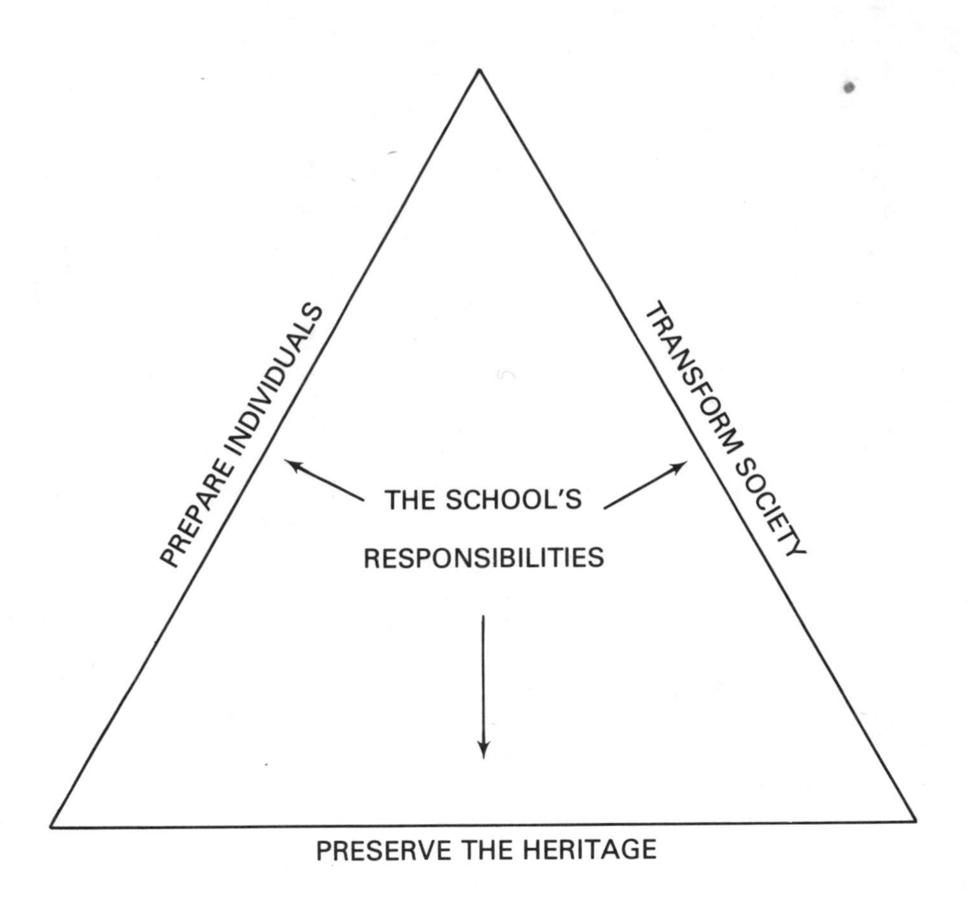

Figure 3

ally willing to face long-time societal challenges and become directly involved and emotionally committed to meeting them.

This role is a "critical intelligence" approach with a futuristic orientation, not an indoctrinating or a crusading one. Surely it is a third and equally imperative responsibility of education in general, and of school and college instructional programs in particular. For it is in those formative years of childhood and youth that sound foundations can be laid upon which youth and adult societal transformation activities may be firmly based. Civic progress can flourish on hopes for the future far more effectively than upon memories of the past. And for educators, especially, the message is explicit: America's Third Century demands a school curriculum which creatively and courageously faces the future, however grim, not the past, however glorious.

How does realistic education help create a better future? Perhaps we can best begin by scanning the historic struggle — carried on by forward-looking educators through generations past — to make school education truly functional. It is at once a discouraging and an inspiring story!

3. HISTORIC PERSPECTIVE

It is important to recognize that true community education is not achieved within a few years. It is a process that must develop slowly and steadily. New community education programs often are a number of activities and programs; nothing more. The crucial test, however, is the direction that is being taken. Are the programs being planned to assure deeper involvement later, or are they planned to provide a service to the individual with no further objectives?

— Jack D. Minzey and Clyde LeTarte,
Community Education: From Program to Process

The subject-centered tradition in curriculum structure remains dominant in most of our schools, just as it has for centuries. Some may consider this fact final evidence that the traditional approach in schooling is inherently superior to all others. More discerning persons, however, will remember that behind the academic tradition lies the enormous and still potent prestige of medieval scholasticism and Renaissance humanism. Yet such prestige, however great, does not necessarily embody guiding values for effective education today.[1]

"Scholasticism" is the term used by historians for the viewpoints and methods of the Christian thinkers and teachers of the Middle Ages. Their chief philosophic problem was to harmonize reason with theology, logic with faith. Although scholasticism systematized theology and produced some subtle minds, the disputations of these medieval schoolmen tended to become empty quibbling, divorced from the concerns of real life, artificial and academic, and ends in themselves.

With the Renaissance came the notion that truth is something to be discovered, to be achieved, not something finally revealed and decreed by authority. In such fields as philosophy, art, politics, science, religion and education, the authoritarian traditions were newly challenged. This age turned its gaze from heaven to earth. In education, literature and languages began to displace theology and logic as areas of curricular concern. Yet, these classical humanists soon developed a pedantic preoccupation with words as such. Immersed in problems of literary form and structure, they did little more than substitute a study of philology for that of theology. Then, in 1560, Europe saw the invention of the printing press. One result was that, as books became available, the school's task often came to be narrowly conceived as that of transferring printed words into pupils' memories, without much regard for the pupils' individual needs or, even, for the significance of the words themselves.

EARLY VOICES FOR REALISM

In thirteenth century France, Peter of Blois looked hard at the schools of his time and then raised the ever-demanding basic curriculum question:

> What does it profit them (students) to spend their days in these things which neither at home, nor in the army, nor in business, nor in the cloister, nor in political affairs, nor in the church, nor anywhere else are good to anyone — except only in the schools?[2]

Against this barren intellectualism arose a movement known to historians as educational realism. This movement, which is a point of view not an organization, challenged the verbal preoccupations of both scholasticism and humanism. It emphasized the importance of giving the practical aspects of life a more central place in the learning processes of school. Educational realism demanded that the curriculum be concerned with the vital life needs of individuals and of society and that direct sensory experiences with concrete things and with social problems be a major method of learning.

In England, Francis Bacon (1561-1626) laid the scientific foundations for this realistic approach when he formulated the inductive method of reasoning. Bacon did not invent inductive reasoning — that is as old as the human mind — but he was first to show the world that intelligent observation must be a process of generalizing from observed data, rather than one of evaluating specific data according to preselected premises. In doing this, Bacon stimulated the rise of the realistic viewpoint in education, especially through his influence over Jon Amos Comenius (1592-1670).

Comenius, the Moravian "prophet of modern education," applied the inductive principles, contributed by Bacon and other sensory realists, to the problems of the school room. He enunciated, nearly three hundred fifty years ago, many of the basic principles of educational methodology which we today accept so easily and violate so often. These principles include: 1) the liberating goal of education; 2) the crucial role of sense perception in learning; 3) the importance of student interest; 4) the significance of education as guided discovery and problem-solving; and 5) the prime importance of proceeding from the known to the unknown — the near to the remote, the easy to the difficult, the immediate locality to the larger world. Comenius asserted:

> The education I propose includes all that is proper for a man, and is one in which all men who are born into this world should share. . . . Our first wish is that all men should be educated fully to full humanity; not only one individual, nor a few, nor even many, but all men together and single, young and old, rich and poor, of high and lowly birth, men and women — in a word, all whose fate it is to be born human beings; so that at last the whole of the human race may become educated, men of all ages, all conditions, both sexes and all nations.[3]

A century later, in France, Jean Jacques Rousseau (1712-1778) asserted the same concern for life-centered education. He stated:

> In the natural order of things, all men being equal, the vocation common to all is the state of manhood; and whoever is well trained for that cannot fulfill badly any vocation which depends upon it. Whether my pupil be destined for the army, the church, or the bar, matters little to me. Before he can think of adopting the vocation of his parents, nature calls upon him to be a man. How to live is the business I wish to teach him.[4]

Following Rousseau, the Swiss educator Johan Heinrich Pestalozzi (1746-1827) laid the foundation for modern elementary schooling with his emphasis upon the ideal of liberty of firsthand experience as the basis for true learning. Speaking to teachers, he offered the following advice:

> Lead your child out into Nature, teach him on the hilltops and in the valleys. There he will listen better, and the sense of freedom will give him more strength to overcome difficulties. But in these hours of freedom let him be taught by Nature rather than by you. Let him fully realize that she is the real teacher and that you, with your art, do nothing more than walk quietly at her side. Should a bird sing or an insect hum on a leaf, at once stop your walk; bird and insect are teaching him; you may be silent.[5]

In 1859 the English philosopher Herbert Spencer (1820-1903) posed succinctly the central curriculum issue we freely acknowledge but still largely evade. In a provocative essay he declared:

> How to live is the essential question for us. Not how to live in the mere material sense only, but in the widest sense. . . . In what way to treat the body; in what way to treat the mind; in which way to manage our affairs; in what way to bring up a family; in what way to behave as a citizen; in what way to utilize all those sources of happiness which nature supplies — how to use all our faculties to the greatest advantage of ourselves and others — how to live completely? And this being the great thing needful for us to learn, is, in consequence, the great thing which education has to teach. To prepare us for complete living is the function which education

has to discharge; and the only rational mode of judging any education course is to judge in what degree it discharges such function.[6]

Down through the centuries such perceptive persons in Europe did think seriously about traditional school purposes and curricula, did question established goals and programs, did urge realistic and functional reforms. In their own times they were often only voices crying in the educational wilderness, yet their influence upon later school practice was both creative and cumulative.

AMERICAN BEGINNINGS

In our country, in this century, American educators of insight and wisdom have widened these horizons still further. Their impact upon formal education, "the lazy giant," to use Harold Rugg's fine phrase, has been sporadic, but is increasing through the passing years.

The continuing struggles for realism and relevance in education can be partially highlighted chronologically. Only a few milestones can find space here; many others await inclusion in some definitive and as yet unpublished history of the community education movement. All proclaim through varied emphases and efforts that effective learning requires active, satisfying, personal experience with significant aspects of human living.

1890 — Parker's Practice School Started: Francis Parker's school was child-centered, in the current sense of that term, but it was also within itself a small community with children, parents, teachers and administrators all working together. The faculty chose as a central theme: "What knowledge does this class need for its present life?" Parker described both the individual and societal goals: "The social factor in the school is the greatest factor of all . . . the mingling and fusing and blending of each with all gives personal power, and makes the public school a tremendous force for the upbuilding of democracy."[7]

1899 — *School and Society* Published: John Dewey's *School and Society* was the first book to stress the social responsibility of the school to improve the community as well as to educate the child. Dewey counseled "We are apt to look at the school from an individualistic standpoint, as something between teacher and pupil, or between teacher and parent. That which interests us most is naturally the progress made by the individual child of our acquaintance. . . . Yet the range of the outlook needs to be enlarged. What the best and wisest parent wants for his own child, that must the community want for all its children. Any other ideal for our schools is narrow and unlovely; acted upon, it destroys our democracy."[8]

1911 — First Yearbook on Schools as Community Centers: The National Society for the Study of Education issued *The City School as a Community*

Center and *The Rural School as a Community Center.* They described adult lectures in school buildings, vacation use of school playgrounds, evening use of school facilities for recreation, home and school associations, and extension courses. A conclusion was that "The secret of success of the work described seems to have been in bringing the school into touch with the community at as many points as possible, and by having the school relate itself to some form of helpful work that may be appreciated by the community."[9]

1913 — First Book on Community Resources: Joseph K. Hart's *Educational Resources of Village and Rural Communities* perceived the community as the true educational influence. "Within the community there is work that educates and provides for life; within the community are the roots of the cosmopolitanism that marks the truly educated man; within the community there is room for a noble and dignified culture and leisure for all. Let us become aware of our community's resources, physical, social, moral. . . . Let us organize our socially supplementary institution — the school — until it shall adequately reinforce the work of education where it is weak and supply it where it is wanting. So, and only so, will the child become really educated, and the community find education genuine, practical, thorough, and vitally moral . . ."[10]

1918 — "Seven Cardinal Principles" Proclaimed: The essential purpose of public schools, said the Commission on the Reorganization of Secondary Education of the National Education Association, is to help induct the young into the on-going life of society, to help them master the tools and develop the insights and abilities necessary in individual and group living. Schools do not exist to teach subject matter as such. They should teach about the problems of learning to live successfully, wholesomely, and creatively. Although the Seven Principles were suggested as guidelines for high schools, they were soon generalized as the major life areas in which children as well as youths should become as competent as possible. The areas of life concern: health; command of fundamental processes (the 3 R's); worthy home membership; vocational efficiency; civic participation; worthy use of leisure; and ethical character.

1923 — Community Study Curriculum Developed: Ellsworth Collings told how he had organized the life of a one-room rural school around the problems of that community and demonstrated in the process that a project curriculum so structured was academically more effective than the traditional subject-centered pattern, even for the so-called fundamentals. In addition, it enriched the living of the community people as well as of the students by relating the local community to wider affairs outside. Collings put into actual practice the concept we today call the "education-centered community." He believed that the school's "chief mission is to provide opportunity for continuous education of children and parents jointly in the affairs of community life," and that "(1) The school curriculum should be expressed in terms of activities of community life, (2) The school procedure should provide opportunity for boys and girls to pursue activity in the way they normally do in life outside the school, and (3) The school should be the educational center of the community."[11]

1929 — School and Community Education Integrated: Among the very first community schools were two developed by Elsie Clapp; the first in Kentucky, the second, later, in West Virginia. These schools made the living experiences of the people of all ages the specific subject matter of school education. They organized people to meet the urgent work, health and recreation needs of the area. There was no distinction between the school and life outside it. The people of the community came to see that all the life processes of a society are in themselves educative, and they deliberately focused their community enterprises, including local government, in terms of their search for quality education for people of all ages. The school became a true community, and the community itself a school.[12]

1936 — First Superintendent of Education: As part of the Tennessee Valley Authority (TVA) development, the town of Norris, Tennessee, appointed Glenn Kendall as "Superintendent of Education" in designed contrast to the traditional superintendent of schools. That was because education was understood to be far more comprehensive than schooling. As Kendall explained, "The educational philosophy which governs the program has been stated: The aim of education in Norris is to develop healthy, intelligent citizens and happy, socially useful members of a democratic society. . . . The curriculum should be centered around basic areas of human activity. . . . There should be core fields of instruction adjusted to the needs and interests of individuals rather than a definite number of separate subjects. . . . Subject matter should be used as it applies to real life situations; not as having virtue in itself. . . . The curriculum should be society-centered rather than subject-centered. . . . The school should be organized throughout for laboratory procedures, using the community as much as possible for first-hand studies and experience . . ."[13]

1936 — Beginning of the Flint, Michigan, Program: Community schools were initiated under the inspiration and leadership of Frank J. Manley and with the financial assistance of Charles Stewart Mott. Five schools were opened as community centers to provide enrichment and recreational opportunities for youth and adults. Even though these were not the first community schools, the program in Flint has since its inception served as a catalyst and model for community school education. It was the first city system to go the community school route.

Manley is often considered as the father of community education because of his lifelong dedication and leadership in community school education development throughout the nation and in other countries. As he saw it,

"Our program was to make the community school director a part of the community. He developed enthusiasm and interest by talking to the people in the community. Relevancy is the word everybody uses now, but that's what we were trying to do. The idea of passing out balls, bats and basketballs, opening up doors and pouring coffee, was in my way of thinking just a simple Come on folks, come on in and get involved."[14]

1936 — First Book on Community Service Projects: *Youth Serves the Community,* a casebook describing numerous service programs developed by high school students, was produced by Paul R. Hanna. Dynamically he summarized the potential for widespread expansion of such efforts in the future as he looked ahead and envisioned "Children and youth, millions of them the world over, restless with tremendous energies! Communities, thousands of them from Pole to Pole, embracing the conditions and materials from which we may create a far more ideal environment for better living! On the one hand, the great energy of youth requiring only a dynamic purpose to make that force the most constructive factor in social progress. On the other hand, cultures rich in potentialities, needing a great constructive force in order to realize the abundant human life they are capable of providing. To coordinate these two mighty resources — to harness the energy of youth to the task of progressively improving conditions of community life — that is the supreme challenge to educational and social statesmanship."[15]

1938 — Purposes of Education in American Democracy Statement: In the midst of World War II the American Association of School Administrators and the Educational Policies Commission of the National Education Association issued their comprehensive description of "what we think the schools of the United States ought to try to accomplish." They published a four-fold group of desired goals, with supporting subheadings for each:

Self-Realization

The educated person has an appetite for learning . . . can speak the mother tongue clearly . . . read efficiently . . . write effectively . . . solves problems of counting and calculating . . . is skilled in listening and observing . . . understands the basic facts concerning health and disease . . . protects his own health and that of his dependents . . . works to improve the health of the community . . . is participant and spectator in many sports and other pastimes . . . has mental resources for the use of leisure . . . appreciates beauty . . . gives responsible direction to his own life.

Human Relationships

The educated person puts human relationships first . . . enjoys a rich, sincere, and varied social life . . . can work and play with others . . . observes the amenities of social behavior . . . appreciates the family as a social institution . . . conserves family ideals . . . is skilled in homemaking . . . maintains democratic family relationships.

Economic Efficiency

The educated producer knows the satisfaction of good workmanship . . . understands the requirements and opportunities of various jobs . . . has selected his occupation . . . succeeds in his chosen vocation . . . maintains and improves his efficiency . . . appreciates the social value of his work. The educated consumer plans the economics of his own life . . . develops standards for guiding his expenditures . . . is an informed and skillful buyer . . . takes appropriate measures to safeguard his interests.

Civic Responsibility

The educated citizen is sensitive to the disparities of human circumstance . . . acts to correct unsatisfactory conditions . . . seeks to understand social structure and social processes . . . has defenses against propaganda . . . respects honest differences of opinion . . . has a regard for the nation's resources . . . measures scientific advance by its contribution to the general welfare . . . is a cooperating member of the world community . . . respects the law . . . is economically literate . . . accepts his civic duties . . . acts upon an unswerving loyalty to democratic ideals.[16]

1938 — First Book on Community Schools in Action: *The Community School* described in detail the programs and operating principles of nine elementary and secondary schools in the United States. Through case accounts it clarified the essential differences between the community school and the traditional kinds of school programming. Editor Samuel Everett summarized these differences as nine basic issues:

All life is education *vs.* education is gained only in formal institutions of learning;

Education requires participation *vs.* education is adequately gained through studying about life;

Adults and children have fundamental common purposes in both work and play *vs.* adults are primarily concerned with work and children with play;

Public school systems should be primarily concerned with the improvement of community living and improvement of the social order *vs.* school systems should be primarily concerned with passing on the cultural heritage;

The curriculum should receive its social orientation from major problems *vs.* the curriculum oriented in relation to specialized aims of academic subjects;

Public education should be founded upon democratic processes and ideals *vs.* the belief that most children and most adults are incapable of intelligently running their own lives or participating in common group efforts;

Progress in education and in community living best comes through the development of common concerns among individuals and social groups

vs. progress best comes through development of clear-cut social classes and vested interest groups which struggle for survival and dominance;
Public schools should be responsible for the education of both children and adults *vs.* public schools should only be responsible for the education of children;
Teacher-preparatory institutions should prepare youth and adults to carry on a community type of public education *vs.* such institutions should prepare youth and adults to perpetuate academic traditions and practices.[17]

1939 — Sloan Project in Applied Economics: "What would happen if the schools, serving low-income groups where unrealized opportunities exist, built the major part of their programs around the three economic necessities of food, housing, and clothing? What would be the result if somehow the old-time subjets were geared to present realities, if community needs were pointed out, latent possibilities demonstrated, and every glimmer of effort made to translate learning into practice, tactfully encouraged?" Such were the fundamental questions that the state universities of Florida, Kentucky, and Vermont, in cooperation with their respective state departments of education, sought to answer through longtime experimentation, beginning in 1939. New curriculum materials were produced for every grade level, programs developed, and results measured in terms of specific improvement in the standards of living of participating communities, and of academic achievement.[18]

1944 — Community Schools Urged: In its *Education for All American Youth* the Educational Policies Commission boldly described the kinds of life-centered, community high schools that it asserted must be developed everywhere if youth needs were to be met. This was a detailed and comprehensive plan showing how high schools and junior colleges could be transformed in purpose and in program to meet the basic needs of their students, and to capitalize upon the varied abilities of *all* youth, regardless of their individual capabilities, interests, or concerns. In later years the Commission published similar community education-oriented volumes dealing with preschool education, the elementary school, and a further look at the high school situation.[19]

1945 — First State Department of Education Community School Consultant Service: Community education development was the purpose of the Division of School and Community Relations, established in the Washington State Office of Public Instruction. Its function was to provide consultant services to school district administrators, curriculum committees, PTA's, and colleges and universities. Over the five-year period of the Division's existence, twenty-one school districts were helped to design systematic programs of community survey, analysis, resource use, curriculum development, and community study by teachers. These programs included lay participation in policy and program planning.[20]

1945 — First Teacher Education Textbook on Community Education: *School and Community,* authored by Edward G. Olsen and others, explained the philosophy, procedures, problems and developments of community study and service through schools and colleges. Through two editions this volume was continuously in print for twenty-nine years, and was published in Spanish and Japanese language editions. "From many sources one learns that all life is educative, that the democratic school must become definitely concerned with the improvement of community and social living, that the major areas and problems of life should give direction to the curriculum, that functional education requires active participation in constructive community activities, and that in this air age the community must be thought of as local, regional, national, and world-wide in scope."[21]

1949 — National Citizens Commission for the Public Schools Organized: "The problems of public education concern all of us, and it is time for *all* of us to do something about them," said a group of influential lay people as they founded a new education-concerned organization. Its purposes were to stimulate a resurgence of popular interest in the schools, to help local district committees of citizens to work with their boards of education in order to decide what they wanted the schools to do, and how they could help educators do it. The Commission operated for several years as a national clearing house whereby local and state groups could share information.

1953 — Comprehensive Analyses of the Community School: The National Society for the Study of Education published *The Community School* as part of its yearbook. It was written by a small committee chaired by Maurice F. Seay. Reporting both theory and practice, the study defined the community school "as one which offers suitable educational opportunities to all age groups and which fashions learning experiences for both adults and young people out of the unsolved problems of community life." The book provided scholarly scrutiny of the philosophy, nature and functions of the community school, explained the nature of community organization in relation to educational procedures, and reported numerous case studies of community improvement through community school efforts in the United States and in some other countries.[22]

1953 — The Association for Supervision and Curriculum Development of the National Education Association issued *The Modern Community School.* Edited by Edward G. Olsen, this book was the product of ASCD's Committee on the Community School. It emphasized direction, process and procedures in community school programs, best practice, tested principles of development, and a value frame of reference that is educationally sound and dynamic as well as fully democratic. "The community school is seen as a part of the larger pattern of community education in which it is the function of the school to help the whole community identify its needs, set priorities, and organize appropriate educational measures to achieve the goals sought."[23]

1955 — First Book on Community Education Administration: Ernest O. Melby produced *Administering Community Education*, a forthright appeal to school administrators of the nation. "Our basic questions," he asserted, "are something like this: How can teachers and educational administrators function to make a creative impact upon all the various factors in the child's total environment? How can the school be managed so that it not only makes its best contribution to the child's growth and development, but also exercises the best possible influence upon all the other elements of the environment, which should be controlled in desirable directions for the child's greatest possible growth and development? Actually, we are faced with the challenge of building creative communities. . . . We must apply the processes of truly creative education to the entire community."[24]

These milestones as well as many others have led innovative educators along the road from the traditional school of yesterday toward the community education of tomorrow. They know that organized knowledge is our greatest intellectual resource for both personal development and societal improvement, provided that such knowledge is functionally organized to meet life's problems, not mastered as a virtual end in itself. They recognize that child interests and self-expressions are splendid educational springboards to be utilized as such, but that these must never be mistaken for educational goals in themselves. They are deeply aware that practical *methods* of education must be evolved out of the psychological study of child and human nature. They also perceive that valid educational *purposes* can be identified only through sociological analysis of culture patterns, as judged in terms of their demands upon the individual and appraised in light of the highest ethical values of civilization.

SINCE SPUTNIK

The community school concept gained increasing acceptance among American educators and many of their professional organizations between the late 1930s and mid-1950s. Some statements indicative of that increasing support are quoted below. In those decades it seemed to many that just as the progressive education movement of the 1920s had profoundly improved the character of American school education generally, especially on the elementary level, so would the community school movement, which followed, have similar positive and widespread influence.

1926 — National Society for the Study of Education: The curriculum can provide for effective participation in social life, by providing a present life of experiences which increasingly identifies the child with the aims and

activities derived from the analysis of social life as a whole. . . .[25]
1939 — Educational Policies Commission: It is literally shameful that school buildings and adjacent play areas should remain locked and unused except during school hours. . . . Sound educational policy requires that public school properties be opened to public use outside of school hours, subject to such regulation as will safeguard the public interest.[26]
1944 — American Council on Education's Commission on Teacher Education: [It is] imperative that the school should offer children more than book learning in the classrooms. It must, indeed, make use of all of the community's resources for providing children with direct and valuable contacts with environmental reality.[27]
1947 — American Association of School Administrators: The schools in all types of communities — rural, town, and large city — must address themselves to the task of improving the level of community life in the areas which they serve. The range and depth of firsthand experiences in community living should be increased through the school program. . . . The present practice of making "school studies" come first and community experiences second should be reversed.[28]
1949 — Association for Supervision and Curriculum Development: Concern for social action does not mean neglect of what is traditionally regarded as "the fundamentals." In fact, social action makes tool skills more important than ever because they are used for an obviously worthwhile purpose.[29]
1954 — Educational Policies Commission: The Educational Policies Commission believes that public schools should become vital forces in helping to build better local communities. . . . It believes that laymen and professional educators alike should use the resources of the school to bring about stronger community life. It believes that the community-building role of the school is a tremendously important one in the last half of the twentieth century.[30]
1957 — American Association of School Administrators: The school is no longer a thing apart from the community; it is a part of the community. . . . No teacher can be doctor, lawyer, businessman, judge, major, nurse, economist, musician, pilot, world traveler, octogenarian, horticulturist, and photographer. But all these are waiting just beyond the doors of the school. Bringing this world of reality into the classroom at the right time and under the right conditions is one way to inspire children and to improve learning.[31]

But then came 4 October 1957, the day when Soviet Russia's first sputnik was hurled into earth orbit. The beeping of that basketball-sized satellite rudely punctured American complacency and deeply wounded national pride. We just *knew* that America's technology would never be surpassed. In our emotional writhings we sought and found a scapegoat: the public schools. *They* were to blame! And they were widely blamed for their alleged failures to teach students enough science and math to keep us technologically supreme. "Back to the fundamentals!" was the critics' battle cry. Science, math and foreign languages came to the fore. Federal financing for these special subjects was quickly authorized, and university academic specialists were assembled to design new mathematics, science, and language curricula for elementary and secondary education. The total impact upon the schools was a virtual reversal of the developing trend toward community school education. The mounting impetus of three decades was largely lost. The barely emerging life-concerns curriculum orientation was quietly superceded. The whole traditional, academic-subject curriculum pattern was again entrenched.

In the 1960s the United States entered the so-called space race and by the end of the decade had American astronauts walking on the moon. As a nation we recovered our technological confidence. But at the same time we became interracially more hostile as the Black human rights struggle was intensified. Frightened by our human relations failures, as exposed by widespread urban rioting and campus-protest demonstrations, we began to spend billions of tax dollars to help the disadvantaged, especially in the city ghettos. Federally financed or assisted urban renewal projects legally required that community improvement planning be done jointly by representatives of the poor, social agencies, labor, business, government, *and* schools. With that necessarily cooperative crusade came awareness that neither communities nor schools could possibly do the job alone; all must work together in close and continuing partnership.

Though much of the Great Society effort was abandoned by the Nixon Administration, a residual effect was a renewal of professional and public interest in community school education. Here are a few notable milestones of that renewed development.

1963 — Mott Inter-University Clinical Preparation Programs: This year marked the development of a training program that has had far-reaching effect on the continued growth of community education. Seven Michigan colleges and universities, through the financial assistance of the Charles Stewart Mott Foundation, initiated a consortium for the training of community education leaders. About seventy men and women were selected each year through a national, and sometimes international, search for potential community education leaders. These persons received one-year fellowships to study at the doctorate, specialist, or master's degree level in Flint, Michigan, under the direction of the consortium. This program continued until 1974 when it was replaced by a national training program involving an even greater number of participating institutions.

1966 — Formation of the National Community ~~School~~ Education Association: This new professional organization was designed for the "improvement and expansion of the community school philosophy as an integral and necessary part of the educational process.'' In 1973 the word ''School'' was dropped from the name to emphasize the total community orientation rather than the much more limited lighted schoolhouse idea earlier associated with the community school concept. The NCEA is open to any person interested in promoting and supporting community education. It serves both as a professional association and as a clearing house for exchange of ideas, sharing of experiences, stimulation of enthusiasm, and promotion of program endeavors. (For additional information, see Appendix A, Number 4.)

1967 — National Commission on Resources for Youth Established: The Commission is a nonprofit organization which researches, promotes, and develops models of programs in which young people assume rewarding and responsible roles. In 1971 it began publication of its *Resources for Youth Newsletter* which now reaches over 20 thousand educators, youth workers, and other concerned people. ''Our country desperately needs the caring and human services that youth can offer. It is an ironic fact that while we face tremendous problems, we also have in abundance the means to overcome these problems. . . . What seems lacking is the *commitment* to change the present way of life and enough people capable of providing *leadership* to do this.[32]

1968 — Civil Disorders Commission Urged School Use as Community Centers: During the riots of the late 1960s the National Advisory Commission on Civil Disorders surveyed our troubled nation and as part of its recommendations advised that ''School facilities should be available after normal school hours for a variety of community service functions, delivery of social services by local agencies (including health and welfare), adult and community training and education programs, community meetings, recreational and cultural activities. Decentralization and the establishment of Parents Advisory Councils will afford the community a means through which to communicate needs for such services and to play an active role in shaping activities. . . . This approach will encourage ghetto residents to regard their schools not as alien institutions but as vital community centers.[33]

1969 — First State Financing for Community Schools: Michigan was the first state to appropriate funds to school districts for partial salaries of community school leaders. This financial aid was provided on a matching basis, thus serving as incentive funding. Since then several other states have passed enabling legislation and provided money for community school development. Most followed the Michigan model.

1969 — ''High School Without Walls'' Opened: The Parkway School in Philadelphia became fully community-centered in its whole educational purpose and program. This was a school where students were assigned to work in the city's many organizations and agencies, thereby learning firsthand about important concerns and problems of living. A few years later a similar school, the John F. Kennedy High School, was established in Chicago.

1970 — First State Community Education Association: Michigan was first to organize a state-wide professional group whose purpose, like that of the National Community Education Association, was to stimulate, promote, assist, and strengthen community education developments within its own borders. More than a dozen other states followed suit; in most of them those state associations are flourishing.

1971 — National Center for Community Education: The National Center was an outgrowth of the Mott Inter-University Clinical Preparation Program. The Center changed its focus in 1974 from a year-long training endeavor to one of providing one- and two-week concentrated programs for potential leaders identified by the seventy-one Centers for Community Education across the nation.

1971 — *Community Education Journal:* Richard C. Pendell, owner of the Pendell Publishing Company in Midland, Michigan, began publication of the *Community Education Journal* as the semi-official journal of the National Community Education Association. Five basic purposes were defined in its first issue: "(1) To communicate in as articulate a manner as possible with professional and lay persons about Community Education, (2) To serve as a forum for innovative models in Community Education, (3) To support programs where there is dedication to the preparation of community educators, (4) To serve as a vehicle for the dissemination of scholarly research findings in Community Education, and (5) To further the integration of human and physical resources with the ever-emerging educational programs in a community."[34]

1971 — National P.T.A. Endorsed Community Education: "The P.T.A. recognizes that the learning process is a continuing one, that it is lifelong and involves the total community. The community school provides learning opportunities for all people of all ages at all times. The philosophic principle that the public schools belong to the people may become a reality under the community school program, as people of all ages . . . make the school a part of their lives by continuing participation in programs of their own choosing. The community school may be the vehicle for realizing the full potential of every individual.

"The community school makes maximum use of all available resources, both human and material, in carrying out its program. It develops its curriculum and activities from continuous study of people's basic needs, and involves citizens in that development."[35]

1972 — U. S. Jaycees Support Community Education: The national Board of Directors of the Jaycees explored the concept and programs of community education, identified its salient advantages, and then officially: "Resolved, that the United States Jaycees extend their national support for the further development and expansion of the community education philosophy as it seeks, through the medium of the community school, to promote the increased use of existing school facilities, equipment, and personnel for educational, recreational, social, cultural, and civic activities in response to community needs and wants as determined by the people through their local community school staff and its local council.''[36]

1972 — First University Chair for Community Education: Florida Atlantic University established the first endowed professorship of community education.

1973 — National League of Cities Supports Community Education: The National League of Cities includes in its membership fifty state municipal leagues and their member cities, cities with populations over 30 thousand, the ten largest cities in each state, and all state capitals - almost 15 thousand member cities in all. Its National Municipal Policy statement of 1973 noted that ''While the educational system must constantly strive to improve the quality of its programs, individual schools must reflect the needs of the community they exist to serve.

''Local governments and school districts should make schools a center of community activity by having school facilities available year round and during and after normal school hours for a variety of community service functions, delivery of school services by local agencies, adult and community training and educational programs, community meetings and recreational and cultural activities.''[37]

1974 — First International Conference on Community Education: Held jointly in Las Cruces, New Mexico, and Juarez, Mexico, the conference was attended by representatives from Canada, Colombia, Guatemala, Mexico, the Philippine Islands, Puerto Rico, Scotland, and the United States.

1974 — First Federal Legislation to Support Community Education: President Gerald Ford signed the ''Community Schools Act of 1974'' which said in part that ''The school, as the primary educational institution of the community, is most effective when the school involves the people of that community in a program designed to fulfill their education needs . . . '' Funds were appropriated, and a national Community Education Advisory Council was authorized.

1975 — Office for Community Education Established at the United States Office of Education: Commissioner of Education, Terrel H. Bell, instituted an office for community education to assist in the growth and development of community education. Staff members of the office are responsible for management of federal funds appropriated for community education, and as a communications link with local school districts and state departments of education.

The announcement of this office was made by the Commissioner at the inaugural meeting of the National Advisory Committee for Community

Education. This council, consisting of leaders from throughout the nation, serves in advisory capacity to the Commissioner and his staff.

1975 — International Association of Community Educators Organized: An international association for community educators was formally established at the Second Annual International Community Education Conference. Delegates from twenty-three countries and cultures, assembled in Juarez, Mexico; El Paso, Texas; and Las Cruces, New Mexico, authorized the establishment of an international council to act as an "implementation committee for the embryonic International Association of Community Educators." It is the responsibility of the committee, working with others of the Association, to develop a plan of governance and structure for ratification by the membership in 1976, at its third annual conference scheduled for Seattle, Washington, and in Vancouver, British Columbia. (For additional information, see Appendix A, Number 8.)

These and many other events are indeed milestones in the growth of community education. The really important result of these and other noteworthy advances, in part at least, is that during recent years educational leaders have evolved new and basically different philosophies of school education in its relation to community life and needs. Those fundamental outlooks and orientations, themselves changing through the years, have been developmental in character and are now hopeful portents for the future.

CHANGING SCHOOL ORIENTATIONS

Several school change orientations will be examined in terms of their wide significance for modern education. It should be borne in mind that these are capsulated summaries and hence are necessarily oversimplified. In their essences, however, they are contrastingly dominant orientations held by varied school and community leaders who determine educational policies today. Resultant educational programs now in operation reflect those orientations. Sometimes two or more of them are present in different aspects of the same school program.

What Is Education?

The old, familiar traditional school considered education to be the 3-R skills plus a reservoir of *stored knowledge*. The mind was thought to be something like the gasoline tank of a car; it could be filled with information at the knowledge pump called school and thereafter drawn upon as needed. To be sure, much of the information thus dispensed was obviously nonfunctional at the time. That was of no import to the conventional teachers and parents, all of whom blandly believed that such learning would either come in handy at some later stage of school or life, or would discipline the mind and so strengthen it generally.

During the early decades of this century, the stored knowledge philosophy came under increasing professional criticism and rejection. Careful studies of the learning process demonstrated that the mind is like neither a tank to be filled nor a muscle to be exercised. The laws of learning were discovered and formulated, among them being that of use and disuse: what is learned and then *used* will be long remembered, but what is learned and not used will be quickly forgotten. Child growth studies brought a widening recognition that mental development is but one aspect of human personality. Physical, emotional, and ethical growth are of equal importance.

From this concerned awareness the progressive education philosophy emerged and became influential in the 1920s and early 1930s. Rooted deeply in the earlier teaching of Rousseau, Pestalozzi, Froebel and Parker, this child-centered orientation was powerfully argued and publicized by the writings of John Dewey, William Heard Kilpatrick, Harold Rugg and other influential educators between World Wars I and II. They rejected the traditional stored knowledge concept and espoused instead the idea of *personality growth* as the central goal of education. Yet, vital as this philosophy was and is, its emphasis upon children as children left it in a kind of social vacuum — largely oblivious to the outside social pressures and out-of-school life experiences that so often distort and destroy personality development. That fatal defect became obvious to many in the 1930s with the onset of the Great Depression and the rise of bestial fascist governments in Germany and Italy.

Today we know that all life educates, consciously or subliminally, creatively or destructively, and that education should therefore become a lifelong process of functional learning experiences which help learners develop genuine *competence in living*. This is the philosophy of community education.

What Is the School's Responsibility?

The old answer to the question of school responsibility was simple: *transmit the heritage,* at least that part of it considered to be important to the educated person. The traditional school said, in effect, fit children and youth into the fixed curriculum of academic subjects. If they do not care or cannot cope with it, that is too bad. Insidiously force them out, or openly expel them if school attendance laws permit. Otherwise, put "him" in shop courses and "her" in home economics and hope for the best.

Then came the progressive educators. They organized experimental schools about their child-centered orientation. They believed that the primary task of the school was to *stimulate student interests,* provide for their explorations in and expressions of those interests, and thus assist in desirable personality growth. Be it the Aztecs, earthworms, poetry, ethnic history, or whatever, the school should help students follow their own interests wherever they might lead and then try somehow to get them interested in something else more academic.

Community educators now affirm the central values of both those earlier goal concepts but know also that we must critically re-examine the whole educational process and program in light of the school's basic responsibility to help *improve the quality of living* in the local community, region, nation and the world, as well as in the personal life of the individual learner. Because people have been educated, they should be better people. They should be healthier; they should be stronger; they should be emotionally more stable; they should be more effective citizens, parents, and workers. And we should be able to develop a better society through school education — one that is concerned about social problems as well as personal needs — always providing that such school education is functionally life-centered. This, too, is part of the philosophy of community education.

What Should Citizen Participation Be?

In the past the negative challenge, *"Keep Out,"* expressed the general attitude of most school board members, administrators and teachers toward people who criticized or otherwise indicated concern about what was going on in the schools. "We are trained experts in education," they typically thought even if they were wise enough not to say it openly. "We know what is best, and we do things that way. Just give us our budget money and leave us alone."

Such condescending aloofness proved self-defeating. Voters found their tax bills climbing ever higher, and increasingly they became suspicious of what schools were doing. Attacks on the school mounted, especially from right-wing organizations. In an attempt to recoup their posture with the public, American Education Week, back-to-school nights and other forms of public relations appeals were established; for example, American Education Week has been sponsored since 1920 by the American Legion, the National Congress of Parents and Teachers, the National Education Association, and the United States Office of Education. The "Keep Out" syndrome was changed to that of *"Come See."* Come into our schools and see what we are doing (*our* schools - what *we* are doing), and then give us more money so we can do it better!

This still-existing possessive attitude is not working either. School tax and bond issues fail time after time. When this happens, all that most conventional school people can think to do is tighten the fiscal belt, seek a date for another election, and mount a more intensive campaign of informational publicity.

Some school leaders, however, are deeply aware that a basically new attitude and policy approach must now permeate their practice. They know they must bring to an end whatever elements of the "Keep Out" fixation still remain. They realize that as public relations the "Come See" strategy is also increasingly ineffective. They perceive that in these tumultuous times they must move forward to a new and truly workable community policy: one epitomized in the fine phrase *Let's Plan Together for Quality Education.*

Educators are fast recognizing that education is a community-wide as well as a school responsibility, that community groups and individuals can serve well as two-way channels of communication between school and community, and that people generally "care when they share." Education-concerned citizens as well as school board members and administrators are coming to appreciate the first principle of successful school policy-making: If you want people to support a potential new program, be sure that they understand its value and share with personal satisfaction in the planning, development, operation, evaluation, and continuous replanning. A school administrator's major responsibility is to recruit a good cross section of the citizenry as educational planners and participators.

As the American Association of School administrators stated thirty years ago, "Active lay participation in developing school policies is undoubtedly one of the most effect ways to bring the whole community to the realization that it has a stake in the whole educational enterprise."[38]

Citizen participation is indeed the heart and soul of the community education philosophy.

How Should Curriculum Be structured?

The traditional school curriculum is still almost standard practice. The familiar *discipline subjects* prevail, all the way from algebra to zoology; each one separate from the others and all prepackaged in textbooks and teachers' guides. Today's alternative or free schools attempt to satisfy *personal interests* through varied projects and units of work, each developed out of and organized around individual and small-group concerns of the moment.

But in the community education approach now urgently needed, the curriculum should be flexibly structured about the *enduring life concerns* of human beings everywhere. These concerns, with their attendant problems, are those of earning a living, communicating ideas and feelings, enjoying recreation, finding self-identity, relating harmoniously with other persons, and the like. With the discipline subjects as resource areas and with personal interests as immediate motivators, this emerging approach to the issue of effective curriculum framework is our best hope for creating truly functional education as a process and a program. Until the heart of the curriculum is essentially life centered, we will not have achieved true community education.

DRAMA OF DEVELOPMENT

It is not easy for any of us to think broadly, deeply and fundamentally about the problems of good education. It is so much simpler for board members, citizen councils, school administrators and teachers to tinker with the elements of planned education than it is to re-create its basic structure. It is quite easy to reshuffle the independently respectable variables of the traditional school curriculum. It is very hard, emotionally as well as intellectually, to base our thinking upon the real needs of real people living in the real worlds of specific communities, all tied to the wider world outside. It is hard, very hard, to think clearly and boldly about our really "sacred cow," the Curriculum. But rethink we must, redesign we must, reconstruct we must, if we hope to educate children, older youths and adults to live their lives fulfillingly.

Perhaps it may help at this point to envision the drama of elementary and secondary school education in our century as though it were a theater play in three acts. In a sense, two acts have already been played but continue to be performed. In terms of historic perspective, the curtain is just now going up for the third act. We, ourselves, are on the stage as playwrights as well as performers.

The first two acts have shown us the trend of schooling, the culmination of events and the probable outcomes if present trends continue. But what will actually happen in the third act will depend very much upon what we decide should happen. The educational drama presented in Figure 4 contrasts these three thrusts.

Act I portrays the traditional school, largely indifferent to its communities. This school thought of education as a process of storing up book knowledge. Institutionally, it was unconcerned about either student interests or human needs; it sought mainly to cover specified subject fields within the time spans allowed. Toward the public its typical attitude was "Keep Out."

Act II portrays the progressive, alternative, or free school, awakening to the community. It brought in resource people to enrich and vitalize the classroom teaching. It took students out on field trips to see for themselves how life goes on in the factory, on the farm, in town meetings, and the like. Yet this school also was limited in effectiveness because it conceived of education primarily as a process of individual personality growth. It was much concerned with student interests and little concerned about social needs. Toward the general public, its fundamental attitude was "Come and see what we are doing with your children in our school."

Act III, just now beginning, presents community education as the next great stage in American education, public and private. In essence, community education is the philosophy and process in which both children and adults learn to use the tools of learning to best advantage. Together they utilize the educative process as a lifelong dynamic means to improve quality of living in their own lives and in all relationships with others. The school makes of the community itself a living laboratory for learning to stimulate individual growth through active, personal participation in community problem-solving. It also uses school building facilities as community centers for educational activities by people of all ages and interests throughout the entire year. Accepting its responsibility to work cooperatively with all other community agencies, the community school seeks continuous counsel of community members in formulating its policies, its programs, and in evaluating its results. This school widely expands the boundaries of democratic freedom for students and all others involved. It organizes its planned curriculum directly around the enduring life processes and personal concerns of human beings today and for tomorrow. Toward the general public its general attitude is "Let's work together to educate for better living and to create a better world."

Yes, we have come a long way in formulating our ideas of what education is and should be, the roles that can be fulfilled by our educational institutions, the need for systematic involvement of community members in the educative process, and an appropriate curriculum structure. The composite result is that in some fifty years we have moved, in advanced thinking if not in practice, from support of the traditional school with its knowledge-set-out-to-be-learned philosophy, through the progressive or alternative school with its individual-interests-to-be-expressed approach, and are now coming to accept the concept of community education, designed to improve quality-of-human-living through personal and community problem-solving.

Our examination of this transition draws us to the following twin conclusions:

True education is knowledge-in-ethical action;

Education is too important an enterprise to be left entirely to educators.

What we are going to *do* about these conclusions is a continuing and exciting challenge to each of us; *To each of us.*

Some assurance in meeting that challenge may be found in the most promising development of our times: *community education.*

DRAMA OF AMERICAN SCHOOL EDUCATION PHILOSOPHY IN THE TWENTIETH CENTURY *

MAJOR CHARACTERISTICS OF EACH SCHOOL	Act I TRADITIONAL SCHOOL	Act II PROGRESSIVE or ALTERNATIVE SCHOOL	Act III COMMUNITY EDUCATION SCHOOL
Dominant Goal	Literacy, culture, vocational skills	Self-expression, personality growth	Better living, individual and intergroup
Administrative Orientation	Authoritarian	Permissive	Democratic
Central Focus	On books	On children and youth	On life concerns
Basic Method	Exposition, memorization, recitation, examination	Creative expression of personal interests	Problem-solving to meet personal, community and societal needs
Learning Values	Deferred	Immediate	Both Immediate and Deferred
Idea of Human Nature	Genetically evil	Genetically good	Genetically dynamic
Idea of Discipline	Crack down	Loosen up	Decide together
Curriculum Structure	Academic subjects	Project activities	Concerns of living
Relation with Local Community	Ignored	Studied	Improved
PHILOSOPHIC TREND IN THIS CENTURY	**from** Education = stored knowledge and skills	**through** Education = creative self-expression	**into** Education = actual improvement in living

*This chart adapted from *School and Community* by Edward G. Olsen and Others, Prentice-Hall, 1945, 1954. Used by permission.

Figure 4

4. COMMUNITY EDUCATION: PRESENT AND FUTURE

Community education has the potential to improve man's way of life. It is believed that community education has the power to:

Bring about a rebirth of people's faith in themselves and in society — to replace resignation with hope.

Help people overcome such barriers to social progress as bigotry, prejudice, indifference, and intolerance.

Establish unity of purpose on the part of people in the community.

Relate appropriately to the efforts of the home, the school, and the community in the development of each individual.

Neutralize the fragmenting influences in the community.

Help people gain maximum return on their common investment in school buildings and facilities.

Bring about a united front for the solution of serious social problems.

— W. Fred Totten, *The Power of Community Education*

Today's thinking about community education culminates the contributions of hundreds of writers and practitioners, a few of whom have been identified in preceding chapters. Although this educational philosophy has an extensive heritage, it is still largely unknown to most teachers, students, supervisors, curriculum specialists, administrators, board members, and citizens in general. Among those who do know about it, there is confusion as to what community education really is, what its parameters are, and how it differs from community schools, adult education, compensatory education, and the like. This chapter will describe current concepts of community education, examine its basic major components, and develop a better understanding of the concept and its potential for the future.

COMMON MISCONCEPTIONS

Any attempt to define a comprehensive concept risks the likelihood of sparking a variety of misunderstandings about it. Community education is certainly no exception. As in the fable of the blind men and the elephant, it is easy to touch one part of the whole and then confidently assume that the whole is essentially like that one part. Such inaccuracies are based on the limitations of tunnel vision. We tend to view the whole of any situation through the greatly limited perspective of our individual personal experience.

Very often even those who perceive themselves as community educators make the mistake of narrowly limiting their conceptual thinking by considering the part of the total most familiar to them as adequate representation of the whole. Minzey and LeTarte point out that "Many activities have been falsely labeled as Community Education, and many Community Education persons have promoted as Community Education things which fall short of the complete definition. Consequently, Community Educators have frequently had to defend their existence in the light of false conceptions and misunderstandings about the true meaning of Community Education and its potential."[1]

Misconception: That community education is the after-school and evening program offerings of school systems and/or community colleges.

Community education is often perceived as those courses and activities that are administered by either a community school coordinator, community school director, or community college/community services director. Many times it is also thought of as those courses and activities which are provided for noncredit and which do not require certificated teachers. Basically, then, community education is often erroneously perceived as an extension of the school day beyond the regular instructional program of that institution. Frequently, this is characterized as the lighted school wherein lighting of darkened halls allows use of the school by people of all ages to pursue their special interests. This is surely one important aspect of the concept. However, it is merely a small part of the whole idea.

Misconception: That community education is synonymous with adult education.

Sometimes the concept is perceived as adult education extended beyond high school completion and adult basic education endeavors of a school system. At other times, it has been seen as the act of providing various learning experiences to community members sixteen years of age and older.

It is also envisioned by some as adult offerings in a neighborhood school building, rather than at an adult education center. Finally, it is occasionally regarded as merely adult education under a new label or identity. Of course adult education is an important aspect of community education; but it is only one aspect.

Misconception: That community education is a means to deliver various forms of compensatory education designed to meet specific needs of youth and adults.

Many of the federal, state, and local funds utilized by community educators have had target populations: children entering school but lacking basic readiness; those deficient in reading, writing and mathematics skills; senior citizens; and people of varied ages who lack vocational literacy and other needed job competencies. Community education does include such commendable endeavors, but its focus is not limited to particular segments of the population. Louis J. Tasse said it well when he explained:

> The community school program is not a program for poor people. It is not a program for black people. It is not a program for old people. It is not an adult education program. The community school is a program for people — *All People.* It is people reaching out to improve themselves and their community. It's a process of schools becoming what the people involved in them are becoming. It's change in a time of change![2]

Misconception: That community education is a new name for the old neighborhood school.

That neighborhood school, historic in the United States as the little red schoolhouse, focuses on the immediate geographic vicinity and attempts to meet the needs of the population there. Community education deeply shares this concern to serve the local area people, but it does not limit its efforts to the school attendance area or within the school building itself. Community education uses the neighborhood school facilities and equipment as a central service center. It also pursues the larger goal of developing a functional educational process to improve the quality of living, both individual and societal, through cooperative planning by involved citizens and school people.

One further observation is in order here. In some communities the neighborhood school has been used as an emotionalized slogan to defeat racial desegregation. Like "law and order" and "crime in the streets," the "neighborhood school" is often a pious euphemism to defend the practice of racial residential segregation. Recent violent controversies over school busing make that obvious in view of the fact that hundreds of thousands of rural children have been bused in this nation for some fifty years, with parental approval and without significant objections.

Community education and the neighborhood school are by no means synonymous, even though both share in the desire to utilize all local school facilities effectively.

Misconception: That academic learning and education are the same.

How often an obituary states that John Jones, deceased, finished his education in 1936 (or whenever)! Many people perceive book studies as the focal point of education, with all other types and avenues of learning as markedly less important. Yet we know that much and perhaps most of a person's education comes through family relationships, mass media, peer groups, religious institutions and the like. For better or worse, whether by design or not, such agencies are powerful educators.

Educational nomenclature should be put in proper perspective, and it should be recognized that learning is a lifelong process — that is, one continuous process, with input from many and highly varied sources. Beginning at birth, or before, as some experts believe, and ending only with death, learning is by no means restricted to schools and colleges and to the academic subjects taught within them.

Misconception: That community schools and community education are identical.

They are by no means identical. To use them so is to confuse further our understanding of both. *The community school focuses upon school* as the center of education — upon a building or complex of the kind commonly called a school. This is a more or less conventional schoolhouse within which varied educative activities are conducted, especially for adults, during nonschool times. The teachers are all professionally credentialed for their specific fields. The community is most often involved through use of the school as an educational center for all the people, through the school's use of community educative resources, and through the efforts of a school-community coordinating council.

On the other hand, community education is a broader concept because it goes far beyond schooling.

Community education focuses primarily upon the community as the source and center of education — upon all its relevant sites, institutions, agencies, organizations, and people. The school becomes essentially a place for cooperative planning of significant education experiences in the community (local-world), and for their reporting and evaluation. Much of the education is sought in the living laboratory called the community. The certificated teacher is primarily a coordinator, interpreter and clarifier of the learning experiences. Other recognized teachers are the noncertificated community members who have much to contribute. These teachers are of all ages, vocations, avocations and backgrounds. Many of them have no certificates whatever.

A town librarian, for example, may also be a teacher of literature since the public library is where the books and other materials are and may be borrowed. A city sanitary engineer may also teach public health. Who knows more about that area than he or she? A radio announcer may teach public speaking; a journalist can help with composition; city council members might discuss political issues; union officials and business executives and consumer spokesmen could analyze consumer problems, and so on. Some years ago a pamphlet titled "Fifty Teachers to a Classroom"[3] explained how community resource people can be utilized in the school; so also did two of Olsen's books.[4] Such teachers should be encouraged to teach in what may be termed their own habitats.

In the education-centered community, contrasted to the community-centered school, teaching is an aspect of many kinds of life activities rather than an exclusive, specialized occupation carried on only in schools and colleges. In the learning resources center (still called "the school") teaching is done, but much of the education will be provided in the outside community. This pattern has already proved its merit in the "high schools without walls" of Philadelphia and Chicago.

Misconception: That community education is a new concept, very recently developed and enunciated.

We have already seen in the previous chapters how erroneous this idea is. Maurice Seay, commenting on the gradual growth of community education, noted that: "The current American concept of Community Education has developed out of three centuries of experience with schools and with non-school agencies that have performed various educational functions for the people of communities."[5]

The evolutionary process of the community education concept might be better appreciated by considering the evolutionary development of something in a technical field, i.e., the development of aircraft.

All the basic principles of physics required to raise such a plane, keep it in flight, and land it again existed in our early 1900 high school physics textbooks. Yet, we did not have jet aircraft in those days. The Wright Brothers managed to put together some of the basic aircraft principles in their historic prototype. Others have since built upon these recognized principles to develop our current jet airplane. Community education is much like that today. It is not a new concept; it is the putting together of basic educational principles worked out and written about for a long time, and which in more recent years received impetus from the Charles Stewart Mott Foundation and the community of Flint, Michigan.

Community education is a synthesizing and developing concept. Our current knowledge of its potential is much like coming into a movie theater and realizing that one-third of the film has been shown, two-thirds is yet to come, and, most importantly, that the viewer has significant opportunity to help write the remainder of the script.

CAUSES FOR MISCONCEPTIONS

Several possible causes for the common misconceptions discussed above may be identified. Some of these relate to the perception of something that is extremely broad in its very nature. Others relate to role expectations of educational institutions and their respective staff members. Another set of causes centers about the kind of leadership being provided by institutions that have initiated community education endeavors. Doubtless, the major general cause is that already mentioned: the common tendency to perceive a part of the concept as the whole.

This tendency was described by United States Congresswoman Patsy T. Mink of Hawaii, in an address to the first Hawaiian state conference on community education. She assailed the hazard in the following statement:

> Programs which we promote under the broad rubric of Community Education are often mistaken for the concept itself. How many times has Community Education been identified with programs of adult education held at the neighborhood schools, with vocational education programs also held at those schools, or with programs whose main thrust is merely keeping the schoolyard gates unlocked after school hours to let the community citizens use the basketball courts? These are all part of Community Education, yet without the recognition that they are part of the larger whole, a larger concept, they are severely limited and are not instrumental in the creation, nurture and fulfillment of the community spirit.[6]

Role expectations of institutions also contribute to misconceptions about community education. Public schools have been perceived for a long time as agencies whose responsibility it is to provide academic instruction to youth from five through sixteen or eighteen years of age. They have not been considered community-owned institutions which are community staffed and funded to help provide a variety of learning experiences needed by community members of all ages, concerns and interests. Faculty members themselves often contribute to this misconception. *Education II — The Social Imperative* noted this factor:

> Actually the teaching profession has in many cases been the major "roadblock" to the development of Community Education. Many teachers see the community school as a mere addition to the usual K-12 program. It may be viewed as a good addition to the "regular" program. It is sometimes seen as a good program to be paid for by special funds. In many established "community schools" this inadequate perception prevails. The school is "lighted" and open in the evening. Interesting activities are conducted in the afternoon and evening, but the school for children during the day is untouched by the concept.[7]

Clearly, now, both the education profession and community lay people need to discuss the full potential for major changes in the total educational endeavors of schools, rather than continuing the conventional piecemeal operation. Kerensky and Melby say it well:

> What is needed in American education today is not a set of additions or band-aids to the existing traditional system, but rather new forms. These new forms pay less attention to product, means, methods, and instruments, but give more attention to persons, process, ends and ideals . . . . The new education must examine and re-examine existing assumptions. It must set new goals and operate in new dimensions. This will necessitate new roles for lay people, children, teachers and administrators.[8]

Leadership in community education itself has at times contributed and been at fault in perpetuating misconceptions about the concept. Some practitioners have allowed their sources of funding to dictate the programs and services they offer, rather than develop offerings to meet needs that have been systematically identified by community members.

It must be recognized that basic community education, so far as state funding is concerned, has been a "poor peoples' " program. Some money has been provided to assist in leadership staffing, but very little, if any, has been appropriated for programs themselves. As a result, some community education leaders have sought out other available funding sources and proposed program offerings to generate financial aid from those sources. However, the importance of multifunding in community education should not be denigrated; such funding certainly is important and essential. *But, systematic involvement of community members in identifying their wants and needs should determine program services, not the sources of funding sought or received.*

Another cause for misunderstanding the concept relates again to leadership. Some community education leaders become so consumed by the actual organization and administration of recreational, enrichment, adult education, academic and other such programs that they fail to provide the necessary leadership for continued growth and application of community education to all facets and possibilities of the community's educational endeavors.

Others are greatly limited by their own narrow perception of what community education really means. To them, it is not authentic unless it is publicly called "Community Education" or is achieved through a community school staff. This blindness contributes, as already noted, to the many mistaken notions of what community education is and is not.

WHAT, THEN, IS COMMUNITY EDUCATION?

Ernest O. Melby once remarked that "Community Education is such a simple idea that it is hard to talk about." He later commented that he often received requests to define community education. He responded: "Define Community Education? I can't define Community Education. It can't be defined. It can only be described."

Community education *is* difficult to define or even describe, and there exists today a plethora of attempted definitions and descriptions. Are there common denominators among these many definitions and descriptions? In an attempt to answer this driving question, several definitions /descriptions, which are often cited in the literature of the field, will be first noted and then analyzed.

Comprehensive and Dynamic Approach

> Community School Education is a comprehensive and dynamic approach to public education. It is a philosophy that pervades all segments of education programming and directs the thrust of each of them towards the needs of the community. The community school serves as a catalytic agent by providing leadership to mobilize community resources to solve identified community problems. This marshalling of all forces in the community helps to bring about change as the school extends itself to all people.
>
> Community Education affects all children, youth and adults directly and it helps to create an atmosphere and environment in which all men find security and self-confidence, thus enabling them to grow and mature in a community which sees its schools as an integral part of community life.[9]

Extends the Role

> (Community Education is) a process that concerns itself with everything that affects the well-being of all citizens within a given community. This definition extends the role of community education from one of the traditional concept of teaching children to one of identifying the needs, problems, and wants of the community and then assisting in the developing of facilities, programs, staff, and leadership toward improving the entire community.[10]

Serves the Entire Community

> Community Education is a philosophical concept which serves the entire community by providing for all of the educational needs of all its community members. It uses the local school to serve as the catalyst for bringing

community resources to bear on community problems in an effort to develop a positive sense of community, improve community living, and develop the community process toward the end of self-actualization.[11]

Goes All Out

Community Education is a process. Since it is a process it lends itself more toward description than definition. A process is a set of actions or changes in form; a forward movement; a course. Consequently, efforts to define Community Educaion as a product run the risk of delimiting the concept to a static state. One of the crucial elements in Community Education is its openness to dynamics and change.

Community Education at its best educates *all* and mobilizes *all* in its educational process. Its distinguishing characteristic is that it goes all out — it does everything that can be done — it places at the disposal of each child, each person, the sum total of human knowledge and human service. It leaves no stone unturned in an effort to see that every human being has the optimum climate for growth.[12]

Systematic Way of Looking

Community Education is a theoretical construct — a way of viewing education in the community, a systematic way of looking at people and their problems. It is based upon the premise that education can be made relevant to people's needs and that the people affected by education should be involved in decisions about the program. I assume that education should have an impact upon the society it serves.[13]

Achieves A Balance

Community Education is the process that achieves a balance and a use of all institutional forces in the education of the people — all of the people — of the community.[14]

An analysis of these various definitions/descriptions shows that they have several common denominators. Most reflect that community education is a philosophical concept which can be put into operation, and most reflect that the concept is not restricted merely to elementary and secondary school education. Another common denominator in these definitions/descriptions is that community education's purpose is to serve the entire community, regardless of the age of the participants or the nature of the learning experiences desired. Community member involvement in the educational process is a fourth common concern. This involvement in need identification, goal ascertainment, program development, and systematic evaluation is important. Another commonality in these definitions/descriptions is that community members should have the opportunity to participate in various types of learning experiences which are based upon their identified wants and needs. The importance of interinstitutional and agency coordination and cooperation is yet another common element cited. A final common denominator in these definitions /descriptions points out that community education is a concept that emphasizes community problem-solving by maximizing the use of all community resources: human, physical and financial.

MAJOR COMPONENTS OF COMMUNITY EDUCATION

Community education, simply stated, is an *operational philosophy of education and system for community development*. It is comprehensive in scope and of high potential, equally applicable to any organization, association, or agency that provides learning opportunities for community members. It is a philosophy that subscribes to the systematic involvement of community members of all ages in the educational process. It further suggests the maximum utilization of all human, physical and financial resources of a community. It is a philosophy that stresses interinstitutional and agency coordination and cooperation. It recognizes that learning is lifelong and that it is essential that we provide various types of learning experiences for community members, regardless of their ages. It is a philosophy that advocates democratic involvement of community members in problem-solving and stresses that educational curriculum, programs and services should be community-centered. Most importantly, it is a philosophy that can be put into operation.

Each of these major components will be explored in greater depth in the following paragraphs.

Systematic Community Involvement

Currently there is a tremendous gap between what many community members want from their educational system and what they appear to be getting. This gap can be narrowed and bridged only when community members — old and young, rich and poor, white, black, yellow, brown or red, of whatever religious, societal and political convictions, and regardless of their school attainment level — are intimately involved in the community's educational process. It should never be forgotten that this involvement must be realistic and contributive, never merely token in nature.

Citizen involvement need not be unilateral. Community members should work closely with the professional staff in community assessment, to determine where the community *is* and where they want it to *go*. Together they should determine what groups and interests make up their service population and how the people see their wants and needs. Community members of all ages and backgrounds can be involved both directly and indirectly in various procedures for identifying and evaluating needs and concerns. They can think together about broad goals and specific objectives and then cooperatively establish program priorities and decide upon plans of action to be followed. They can share in the development, distribution, and collection of questionnaires, and help with interviewing and in obtaining demographic data from census tract information and other such sources. Finally, community members can play a very important role in both formative and summative evaluation. In formative evaluation, they can share in critical assessment of the evaluative process itself — of needs identification, goal establishment, program development, and the like. In summative appraisal, they can participate in collecting data to determine how well the goals sought have been reached.

This involvement of community members in the educational process by no means diminishes the role and responsibility of the professional educator. Rather, it enhances and extends both. The professional should play a highly significant part in providing facilitative leadership which encourages and supports citizens willing to assume an active role in the comprehensive educational process of the community. Educators must also use their trained insights and skills in the organizing, conducting, and reporting of resultant programs and services.

Systematic community involvement is often achieved through use of community councils. Most often these councils are only advisory in nature; however, in others, community members share in the decision-making. Community member involvement on community councils has existed many years, yet remains a fairly immature science. Unfortunately, many councils have been merely token in nature or were developed to address themselves to specific program areas. Increased federal legislation also brought forth a plethora of community councils.

Community school educators have done an admirable job in the development of community councils whose members are concerned about the real learning needs of youth and adults. Unfortunately, most of these have not addressed themselves to the life-concerns curriculum possibilities of today and tomorrow.

One can hardly over-emphasize the necessity for community councils to become deeply concerned about the *total* educational endeavors of their respective communities and service institutions. The time has come to discontinue having four to ten councils in a school center whose ultimate goals are similar, yet which address themselves to only facets of the total educational enterprise and who do not work in cooperation with one another. Each school center should have a council that is concerned with its center's total endeavors. Such councils would address themselves to the academic, career, vocational, enrichment, recreational, and other categories of learning experiences for community members of all ages. Advisory and decision-making councils at local school centers or at an institution-wide level should be encouraged to address themselves to the *total* endeavors of their respective units. They should also work closely with the various organizations and agencies of their local areas.

Most communities have already developed a multiplicity of service organizations, each pertaining to particular facets of the total educational enterprise and often having no cooperative and sustained contact with each other. The great need is to bring them into cooperation with one another in order for all to gain a perspective on community needs and thereby work more effectively together than each organization is likely to work alone.

Regardless of organized structure, the systematic involvement of citizens is at the very heart of the community education process. It is essential for community members to think together about their desires and needs, to decide together upon resultant educational goals and objectives, and to assist educators in achieving these purposes. Much experience shows that people will give of themselves when they feel that their contribution is real and has meaning.

Maximum Use of All Resources

Another basic component of community education is the maximum possible use of all available resources for the better education of all people. When resources are mentioned, individuals are most likely to have in mind oil, coal, minerals, and other natural elements — and fail to include and recognize human resources as being the most important of them all. In any given square mile of any population area, there are community members who are rich in varied talents and/or past experiences. In every community live many persons with job skills, hobby skills, and other special interests of many kinds. There will also be people from various walks of life, different cultures, varied ethnic and religious backgrounds. Many of these people would enjoy being involved and acting as resource persons, sharing their talents and experiences with others.

Such involvement might find retired business executives assisting people currently managing small businesses; skilled hobbyists might share their talents and techniques in music, photography, art, drama, physical fitness and numerous other interest areas. People who have traveled are often eager to share their experiences, pictures, and artifacts. Persons of other racial, ethnic and nationality backgrounds would gladly share their knowledge of foods and dress, customs and mores', aspirations and frustrations. Those with special job skills may help interested others develop their own technical know-how. Lifelong community residents can be interviewed for their knowledge of the area's history and development. People who have experienced war, poverty, prejudice, or particular periods of crisis in history can share their perceptions to make both history and contemporary human relations issues come alive.

Field trips, community surveys and service projects, work experiences and school-related camping are other very fruitful avenues of realistic education for people of all ages, by people of all ages, and all levels of academic achievement.

Three criteria should govern the selection and utilization of human resources: their quality of experiences in relation to the immediate educational objectives; their ability to communicate their experiences; and their genuine willingness to do so. Age or level of academic achievement should not be a limiting factor in the utilization of community members and neither should past experiences. Their enthusiasm for new areas of interest and willingness to provide voluntary or short-time employment assistance may also prove immensely rewarding.

If there is little doubt that a community's human resources can be more fully utilized, there is no question that its physical resources, and those of the school in particular, can be used more extensively and more imaginatively. Presently schools are in use one-hundred eighty days out of three-hundred sixty-five! Eight hours out of twenty-four! And, even though one-hundred eighty days do appear to be about one half of a year, and eight hours appear to be one third of a day, the actual use is most meager:

$$\frac{1}{2} \times \frac{1}{3} = \frac{1}{6} \text{ or } 17\%$$

It is ironic to realize that a majority of schools across the nation are utilized less than 20 percent of their available time when, simultaneously, taxpayers are being asked to consider increased taxation for additional facilities. Meanwhile, teachers are confronted with large numbers of students at a given limited time, and school overcrowding is a problem felt nearly everywhere. Yet, it is indisputable that no corporate officials could expect to maintain their leadership roles if they operated their facilities during less than 20 percent of potential use time, while requesting their stockholders to build more facilities and asking their employes to continue to endure crowded working conditions because of inflexible scheduling practices.

Some critics will be quick to point out that nighttime hours are included in these school-use percentages. That is right! Some replies to such comments follow.

In the nation there are a number of schools that already offer opportunities during early morning hours (1:00-3:00 a.m.) because this time has been requested by community members (primarily persons from urban areas who are employed on night shifts and wish to participate in some learning experiences when they complete their work).

It is not necessary to propose twenty-four hour utilization. But how about 33 percent utilization? Or 50 percent or 60 percent? Why are so many persons locked into believing that education takes place best between September and June, between the hours of 8:00 a.m. and 4:00 p.m., and on weekdays only? Unfortunately, the answer to these questions is that same magical ingredient that kept the "fiddler on the roof" — tradition! Time off from schooling is still given to harvest the crops when less than 4 percent of our students now are even remotely involved in agricultural endeavors.

Maximum utilization of physical resources is basic to community education. These resources include all school facilities, equipment, furniture, chalkboards, and, yes, even the gymnasiums and athletic fields. All are jointly owned by the community stockholders: namely, the taxpayers and the community members in general. The physical resources of schools (public schools, community colleges, universities, etc.) have been developed, built, and paid for by community members to meet their identified learning needs. It is time indeed to recognize this fact and to break away from the tradition of utilizing them so little for so few, when they could be used so much by so many.

Education institutions, agencies and organizations often proclaim what they could do if only they had more money. Public schools, community colleges, four-year colleges, universities, state departments of education, trade schools, libraries, zoos, museums and arboretums as well as literally dozens of local, state and federal agencies and organizations, (i.e. recreation departments, social and welfare services, health departments, judicial and penal agencies) have listed lack of funds as the reason for not achieving what they wish they could do for community members.

Regrettably, most such institutions operate quite unilaterally — with very little association or cooperation with one another, financially or otherwise. Many seem to have forgotten that the ultimate source of revenue for all public organizations is the taxpayer, good ole Joe Public. The revenues for public school education may come from the right front pocket, while the source of funds for community colleges and universities is the left front pocket. Certain local governmental services obtain their revenues from the left rear pocket, while still other services receive funds from the right rear pocket. Ultimately, however, they all come from the same pair of trousers, worn by the same good ole Joe.

In order to maximize the effective use of limited funds, it is essential for all educationally oriented institutions, agencies, and organizations to work closely together, to complement one another, to cost-share at times, and to work together toward the mutual goal of providing the best services for the total money available. This is a basic component of community education.

Does this mean that all of these units should be merged? Would the autonomy of these organizations that serve particular and limited clientele be watered down or destroyed? The answer to both questions is no. Each institution, agency, and organization can and should maintain its own identity and address itself to specific problems; however, it is time that these community-financed organizations be expected to work in close and continuing cooperation with one another, thus insuring that the taxpayers get the best educational return for the money they have invested.

The term "synergism" probably best describes what could result from maximizing the financial resources available to several local institutions, agencies and organizations. In one application, the term "synergism" refers to the results that are often obtained when one drug is taken in combination with another. The total effects of those drugs when taken in combination are greater than the sum effects that would be anticipated from the drugs taken separately. In other words, in education as in the drug use example, the sum of the whole is often greater than the sum of the parts in isolation.

As summarized by V. M. Kerensky, community educators can be:

> . . . synergists in their efforts to develop cooperative procedures bringing about the combined action of separate agencies toward common goals. The impact of a totally mobilized effort will produce an effect greater than that of any component taken alone. . . . The allocation and distribution of funds at all levels should be accomplished with this basic concept as an operating premise.[15]

In order to make available funds most productive, it is essential to perceive the community member (source of revenue) as the primary focus, rather than the institution itself. The potential for synergistic results is very good if community members and their concerns remain the central focus of combined attention.

Maximum utilization of human, physical and financial resources through interinstitutional and agency coordination and cooperation carries even more potential for synergistic results and is another basic component of community education.

Cooperation and Coordination

Effective cooperation between community organizations, as well as between them and schools and colleges, has been advocated for several decades. Emphasis has been placed upon the residual educational responsibility of formal education, as well as upon school-community coordination. Fifty years ago C. C. Peters clearly stated and explained that residual obligation:

> The School need not itself attempt to give every form of training needed for life. It is only the coordinating and supplementing factor among all the educational agencies. Its function is a distinctly residual one. It must itself do whatever needs to be done but which no other agency is adequately doing. It begins where the other agencies leave off. That involves, on the one hand, that it should not blindly duplicate what other agencies are doing . . . and, on the other hand, it involves that the school should not pass by any sort of training needed for effective future life which no other agency is adequately giving.[16]

Fifteen years later William A. Yeager stressed the pressing need for home, school and community cooperation for better education:

> Education conceived as a cooperative process entails responsibilities upon all of those *concerned in the educational process.* As the eye cannot get along without the hand, neither can the school get along without the home, nor the school or the home without the community.[17]

In 1945 and again in 1954 *School and Community* restated the problem of the school's appropriate role in the total community's educative process:

> The school is society's chief formal agency for the education of children, youth and adults. What, then, is its special responsibility as one among many other educative agencies in the community? The answer is clear: the school's proper role within the total educative process is both residual and coordinative. In its residual role it is obligated to teach all those ideas, skills, appreciations, abilities, attitudes, and ideals which are essential to people's effective living and which they do not acquire through non-school channels. In its coordinative role, the school will lead other community agencies to develop consciously cooperative programs for the more effective and economical education of all people . . . .
>
> All this implies that a school will neither duplicate the desirable educational offerings generally available through other community agencies, nor fail to utilize them to the fullest extent through leadership in coordinating community educational programs. Surely it is clear that effective education for our times requires continuous and cooperative planning on the part of homes, churches, welfare agencies, service clubs, clinics, professional groups, veterans organizations, business associations, labor unions, women's clubs, youth agencies, etc. *and schools.*[18]

Cooperation . . . coordination . . . how imperative are both, yet how slowly they develop! Educating institutions, agencies and organizations do often try to cooperate, even coordinate some of their policies and programs. In their efforts two major types of working relationships can be distinguished. First are those in which each participating organization asks others to extend themselves for its own benefit, but not necessarily for the benefit of all. Thus, some interagency cooperation is merely the *using* of other organizations — a "what you can do for us" type of relationship. In the second type, coordinative efforts are developed that complement all participating groups — a "what can we do to help one another, and, most importantly, our community members" type of relationship. Cooperation and coordination of educative services for mutual benefit is always a basic component of community education.

To illustrate the potential of working together, two examples of interagency cooperation are noted: the first being school grounds — neighborhood community parks joint endeavors — and the second being comprehensive learning opportunities.

People in many local communities want adequate neighborhood parks with picnic grounds, benches, fireplaces, game areas, athletic fields, and buildings for possible indoor activities; yet seldom do such desires come to fruition. The high costs of potential park sites and needed facilities are most often given as the reasons for not developing a system of community parks. However, in these same communities exist dozens of schools with their respective playgrounds/schoolgrounds, buildings, athletic fields, and other facilities. Might these facilities be developed into neighborhood community parks for all the people as well as serving youngsters during the school day? Yes! These facilities could be transformed into neighborhood parks through the cooperation of the community school system, the parks and recreation department, county and municipal governing bodies, and service clubs. Could students of all ages, who are learning building trades, construct park benches and picnic facilities? Would some of the local service clubs cooperate in developing fields, courts, lights, floral gardens, aesthetic sitting areas, and other aspects of such a community endeavor? Could school-age children play a significant role in the redevelopment of schoolgrounds/playgrounds and other facilities for multipurpose use?

Obviously, such endeavors can be realized through cooperation. The combined results far exceed the sum of effects when each organization works separately.

Public schools, community colleges and universities working in close cooperation with one another could provide a continuum of credit and non-credit learning experiences for community members of all ages. Academic, vocational, avocational, recreational and enrichment learning experiences as well as career, social and family learning could be provided all community members through cooperation between these three major types of public educational institutions. In addition to offering a comprehensive set of learning opportunities, could they not also cooperate for a more effective delivery system? Must university and community college courses and workshops always be held on collegiate campuses? Might public schools, which are distributed throughout a community, be utilized for selected community college and university offerings in order to facilitate delivery? Might staff and program cost-sharing be utilized between institutions in order to provide excellent learning opportunities at minimum cost? What other ways can public schools, community colleges and universities cooperate to provide comprehensive learning opportunities and systems of delivery for community members of all ages?

These two examples of cooperation between public-financed organizations serve only as an introduction to the potential of interinstitutional cooperation and coordination, another basic component of community education.

Lifelong Learning Experiences

"Stay in school so you can get a good job!" "I want you to have more than I have had, so get an education!" Out of the sincerity behind such statements has evolved a concept that education is merely a youthful endeavor to prepare for an adult life still to come. Thus, persons typically assume that real learning is something restricted to one small portion of an individual's life. This is nonsense! Learning is a lifelong process! Learning is as basic to the human being as eating and sleeping; learning begins and terminates with life itself. Our current educational system, however, does little to reflect this philosophy of thinking and action.

The operational philosophy of community education is based on the concept that learning *is* a lifelong process and that schools at all levels should help provide various kinds of learning experiences for community members of all ages. Educational institutions should not restrict their goals and programs to one small portion of a person's life, but instead should recognize the significant roles they can play in providing lifelong learning.

What types of learning experiences should they offer? It is a premise of community education that the nature of the learning provided should be based upon the community members' needs and desires. It is essential, then, for educational institutions to develop and utilize valid techniques for assessing wants and needs of community members.

For a long time educators have categorized learning experiences and given them identity labels such as vocational education, academic education, sex education, career education, adult education, health education, social education, civic education, avocational education, enrichment education, recreational education, family education and the like. But what do all of these terms mean? How do they relate to one another.?

All such categories do represent important facets of the total educational picture and, unfortunately, are treated as if they have very little relationship to one another. Are these truly representative categories of human learning? Why are educators so enthralled with labeling and separating various learning experiences as if they were not related and served different clients? Regrettably, formal education appears to be a conglomeration of pieces like the facets on a diamond; each piece shining its message in a different direction (end of analogy — our current system of education is not a jewel!).

Terms, such as those listed above, should be recognized as merely fabricated categories developed by educators. Of course, these terms do facilitate communication, organization and administration. There is no need to eliminate them, but rather to recognize them as descriptors and treat them as such. It is important for educational nomenclature to be placed in its proper perspective and for learning itself to be perceived as a lifelong process — one continuous process! Educational institutions should provide for the lifelong, integrated pursuit of personal enjoyment and competence in all aspects of living.

Community Problem-Solving

The pressing problems of environmental degradation, overpopulation, prejudice and discrimination, poverty, underemployment, urban blight, malnutrition and many others are at heart *human* problems. Most of them have been created or nurtured by people through premeditation, omission, or ignorance. Most of the attempts to attack these problems have failed. As a nation we have tried at times to mandate, legislate and appropriate solutions but, as yet, with very little success.

It is imperative to realize that large numbers of citizens do not know how to go about solving human problems, whether these are societal or individual in nature. Many of them cannot even distinguish between related parts of a problem, or between symptoms and causes.

Most of us have heard the age-old cry, "I'm good at mathematics, but have lots of trouble with word problems." What is this confession really saying? It says that the speaker can manage the rote mechanics of mathematics, but when confronted with narrative challenges he or she has difficulty relating mathematical concepts to those of apples, bushels, pecks, and peaches. Worse yet, it unknowingly states that he or she cannot differentiate between parts of the problem. How, then, can these same people be expected to understand the causes and solutions to deep-rooted, complex and emotionalized human issues such as those mentioned above? How can people be expected to decipher the component parts of a social problem when they cannot work with the relatively simple concepts such as pounds, bushels, and yards?

Health needs illustrate another type of concern confronting our world population. Today, the causes and prevention procedures of 95-98 percent of all physical illnesses are known to medical science. Yet our world population continues to suffer from malaria, cholera, malnutrition, vitamin deficiencies, plague, fevers, and dozens of other illnesses which can be prevented and/or cured. Why is there this extraordinary gap between knowledge and solution? Solutions to the problems exist; yet the problems are not solved! Again, the comment of Harry Elmer Barnes seems appropriate: "We stand with our mechanical foot in an airplane and our social foot in an oxcart and the stretch is becoming painful, not to say dangerous."

Our critical, worldwide human problems must be solved but, in order to achieve this, individuals must first learn the art or science of problem-solving itself. They must learn the skills of distinguishing between component parts of a problem and how to tackle them methodically. Educational institutions must begin to teach democratic problem-solving at an early age and provide increasing opportunities for continued learning and sophistication in it. Only through *real involvement* in *real problems* can these skills be learned.

A second aspect of this community problem-solving discussion relates to democracy. We live in a country with a democratic form of government. We expect each citizen to be committed to this form of government and know how to function within it. Our expectations are good, but our preparation for citizenship is poor. In our schools we truly do not teach "the ins and outs" of living in a democracy. We teach *about* democracy! We emphasize historic heritage, balance of power, equal justice under the law, and so forth, but we do not give students sustained and critical experience with democratic problem-solving itself even within the school, and practically none in the outside community.

If our democracy is to survive even this century, our educational institutions must provide continuous opportunities for the democratic involvement of community members in societal as well as personal problem-solving. As the building block is the lowest common denominator of the building, so is the individual community member the lowest common denominator of our society. We must invest in the individual. Our major problems, regardless of scope, will begin to be solved only when each individual person addresses himself or herself directly to the problem, and does this via the democratic process.

Life-Centered Curriculum

A sixth basic component of community education is to provide a core curriculum throughout the elementary and secondary school years that is structured directly around the major processes and concerns of human living now and in the discernible future. This almost totally neglected yet imperative essential of community education is the central theme of this volume, so the authors will not discuss it further here. The authors would only reiterate their deep conviction that unless the organized curriculum of community school education focuses directly upon the driving societal and personal concerns of our times, it is indefensible.

In summary, the six components of community education identified and discussed in this chapter represent the essential characteristics of this action philosophy. Someday these may be perceived as merely a beginning, a foundation for continued growth. Other major components will be added as community education develops in theory and is tested in expanding practice. But for now it is exciting to realize that each of us can "add his rock to the pyramid."

CURRENT STATUS OF COMMUNITY EDUCATION

In this chapter the philosophy or theory of a concept has been examined. However, this concept is not being developed by theorists alone. Throughout our nation, as well as in other countries, community education is being initiated through public schools, community colleges, universities, county and state departments of public instruction, and other educational agencies. Hundreds of communities are now implementing some aspects of community education and are utilizing a variety of goals and objectives, approaches, organizational and administrative structures, and a plethora of programs and services to achieve their purposes.

No, community education is not being promoted only by theorists; it is being developed systematically through the contributions of practitioners and theorists working together. Community education is truly an *operational philosophy of education* which is now coming widely into practice.

Statistical data about the extent of community education are changing daily. Attempts to describe its growth and development cannot be accurate, because the information is ever-changing. However, since some data are more descriptive than no data, an overview of the current status of community education appears in Appendix A. This overview includes information on school districts, school centers, institutional and agency involvement, growth at state department of education levels, federal and state legislation, college and university centers for community education, national and state associations, and the National Center for Community Education.

THE CHALLENGE

Community education is a philosophy of education with limitless potential for the future. Our challenge as educators and/or community members is to maximize our use of its potential.

Analogous to this is the utilization of crude oil. From this raw oil scientists and business leaders have developed knowledge and methodology to obtain, refine and manufacture such basic commodities as gasoline, resins, fuel oil, fiberglas, kerosene, alcohol, grease, antifreeze, vasoline, medicine, various kinds of plastic, paints, solvents, various organic chemicals, and the many new wonder fibers from which hundreds of clothing, floor covering, and houseware products are made. Yet, that crude oil will probably yield even more products in the future.

Community education has a similar yield potential, but, unlike oil, there exists no limit of essential resources. The basic principles of community education are applicable to the entire instructional program of educational institutions, agencies, and organizations, and should not be restricted to mere facets of educational endeavors.

> To think of community education as a separate program superimposed upon existing schools destroys the concept at its inception. To think in terms of community education as a simple extension of an obsolete educa-

> tional system that has serious problems and is in danger of falling as a result of its own dead weight is also a misconception. Extending the existing educational program is not the answer to a successful community education program until there are dramatic changes in the existing structure of our present day schools. One should not visualize a community school program as frosting placed on the existing educational cake. Community education is "the cake" . . . a new cake. Community education envisions a new educational cake . . . with a new recipe, new ingredients, and totally new dimensions.[19]

The authors agree and assert with full confidence that community education is not frosting. It is an essential and working philosophy designed to produce functional, lifelong, quality education for people of all ages, all backgrounds, all interests, and all concerns. The challenge is to maximize the potential of this concept by developing truly life-centered curricula for people of all ages, interests and needs. Such a life-concerns curriculum will be presented in the chapter to follow.

5. LIFE-CONCERNS CURRICULUM

The challenge today in regard to curriculum change is to establish a process in which multiple forces will be taken into account, yet reasonable decisions as to curriculum will be made. We cannot afford a paralysis created by endless discussion. Nor can it allow confrontation to prevail as the accepted way of making curriculum change. Today in curriculum change we are close to an anarchic situation in which the forces and agents with the most power reign temporarily in an eternal "king-of-the-hill" struggle. We have to develop new ground rules for a wider sharing in curriculum decision-making which utilizes more effective democratic processes than have yet been devised.

Let us hope that educators and citizens of the future recognize . . . the central place that should be occupied by social realities, the needs of individuals, and humane values. If we base our educational programs on social realities, needs, and values, and if we stress integration of knowledge, education may have a fighting chance to make a difference in the quality of the lives of the individuals who inhabit this nation.

— William Van Til, *Curriculum: Quest for Relevance*

We must, through those decision processes, create curricula which are dynamic, which are, above all, viable constructs for life today, for life tomorrow. To that end, the authors suggest these central assumptions concerning community education:

All life educates, not just the school;

The goal of community education is to educate people for better living for a better world;

The school must often lead the community into cooperative development of educational policies and programs, including that of the curriculum;

The major concerns of life today and tomorrow should become the core of the regular school and community college curricula.

It is the intent of this chapter to suggest that the life processes and concerns of human beings become the common core of systematic learning of youth, the core having built-in flexibility so as to function with persons of all kinds of interests and abilities. Within this required core there can be much opportunity for individualization of emphasis and expectation. Around this core can be included academic and special subjects as desired by individuals and small groups. All such conventional "subjects," however, should be electives for those who want them, not barriers against those who do not. And within the proposed curriculum frame, at every stage and every level, there should be plenty of room for the exploration and testing of educational innovations and approaches. Adaptive education, affective education, career education, credit-noncredit systems, differentiated staffing, discovery education, flexible scheduling, group planning, independent study, individualization, inquiry approach, nongrading, open classrooms, tutorial programs, team teaching, cooperative training, alternative programs, year-round schools, and other such concepts and innovative endeavors should be continuously encouraged and tested.

Let this be clearly understood: the present discussion concerns a *core curriculum only*, one requiring between one-third and two-thirds of any student's time. The remainder of the learning time should be available for all sorts of individual and group activities, general work experience, specific career training, community service programs, survey, extended field trips, systematic academic courses, and the like, all with or without credit. During this noncore time, varied academic areas might well be overviewed by means of minicourses designed to provide interest-generating exposure and some basic background for later development. Core and noncore activities alike, however, should stress participatory education, society orientation, illumination of human realities, analysis of values, and constructive community action.

CONCERNS AND CURRICULUM

Newborn children are not concerned about others. However cuddly and delightful, they are still egocentric and unsocialized. Their loudly expressed feelings demonstrate that in their basic assumptions they are centers of the universe. They expect that their environment should respond immediately to all of their demands. So the process of child development is essentially one of socialization; children must learn progressively, often painfully, how to become civilized and human in their thinking, feeling and doing.

As adolescents, they are normally rebellious and questing — rebelling psychologically and physically against adult-world controls and domination, questing for personally satisfying answers to the great concerns of humankind: Who am I? Why am I, I? How do I relate with others? What is this society all about? Why are things the way they are? Why don't "they" make matters better? What is really important in life?

Just as children through their learning must become less egocentric and more socialized, so must adolescents seek their personal identities and create their own life styles and values to live by. In this manner, infants growing into childhood and through adolescence attain mature and responsible patterns of adult living. In this necessary developmental process young people become self-consciously aware of what concerns them the most at different stages of their growth and with varying degrees of insight and sensitivity. In both childhood and adolescence those areas of developmental concern are mostly *individual:* getting along with parents, peers and people generally; fun, money, sex, drugs; finding a career; marrying or not; seeking personal recognition and status; searching for a secure sense of identity and the emotional meaning of selfhood.

But, for many of these youth, especially the brighter, better educated among them, serious *social* concerns develop also: the problems of environmental degradation, overpopulation, malnutrition, disease, exploitation, racism, sexism, materialism, militarism, war, authority, power, social change. Many youth, disillusioned with what they perceive to be uncaring or corrupt adult values and behaviors, become increasingly alienated from all except some in their own age group.

Are not all interests, both individual and societal in nature, the actual life problems of growing up? Are they not the genuine *concerns* that turn young people on, the things they really care about? Growing up is a process of finding for oneself a reasonably satisfying place in the adult world. This means achieving some degree of competence in each of at least four major roles played by every person:

Sex and family role — Getting along with parents, siblings and peers, later finding a fulfilling sexual life, deciding whether to create one's own family;

Productive worker role — Ability and willingness to earn an adequate economic living and wisely to consume goods and services;

Civic role — Obedience to just laws as a minimum; beyond that, active participation, democratically, in local, state, national and world politics;

Self-realization role — Discovering and developing live-with answers to the persistent and lifelong questions confronting each of us, Who am I? What do I want to be like? Where am I going in my life and why?

These four roles, or life careers, are among the basic concerns of all persons, in greater or lesser degree, whether consciously recognized as such, or not. (Some readers may want to equate these four individual roles rather directly with sociologist George Murdock's five sets of norms that are found in some form or other in all societies: Family — the rules and regulations relating to sex and reproduction; Government — the legitimate uses of power; Economy — production and distribution of goods and services; Education — the indoctrination and socialization, particularly of the young; Religion — relationship between man and supernatural.) Such roles are dominant life areas in which children, teenagers and adults feel, think, and act. It is imperative that schools, colleges and other educational institutions and agencies recognize this and direct their efforts toward helping people of all ages, abilities and interests to attain some degree of individual competence in each of these roles, as well as in other significant areas.

But what does the conventional school and college curriculum offer to children, youth and adults? To help them meet their concerns and needs, it offers them chiefly the traditional subjects of study, academically predigested and formally presented, and almost always with a rearview-mirror focus. Almost nowhere are their own life role concerns, interests, and anxieties central in the curriculum, or even included as optional areas for sustained small-group or individual exploration. Is it any wonder that in most schools and colleges intrinsic classroom motivation becomes difficult, even impossible, except for grade-obsessed children of grade-demanding parents? Should it be any surprise if some young people turn toward drugs and other cop-outs or to the rhetoric and even terror tactics of the violent rebels or revolutionists? Is it not increasingly clear to teachers and parents alike that traditional subjects of study often turn many youth off? Should not a long, skeptical assessment be taken of the conventional school curriculum?

Crucially required, especially for the older childhood and teen years, is a basically new approach to the curriculum content and structure problem. We had better stop asking what in the conventional subject areas can somehow be made more directly meaningful to students. Instead, concerned planners should try to find out what are the real and vital concerns felt by each individual that are also of importance to people, communities, regions, nations and our planet, and then they should develop functional curricula based on these concerns. Then, and only then, can the current school crisis begin to be surmounted and the legitimate education demands of our times begin to be met.

LIFE-CENTERED CURRICULUM PROPOSAL[1]

What might happen if alert schools and colleges dared to experiment with a curriculum genuinely life-concerns centered? Such curriculum experimentation would not mean adding to the traditional program a new course or two or some new units of study. Nor would it mean including a few student community activities related to ecology, ethnic prejudice, sex, drugs, safe driving or anything else that is merely tacked on to the regular curriculum. It would mean eliminating from the generally required pattern of studies all the traditional academic studies in their discipline form and would mean substituting for them systematically organized learnings about the enduring life concerns and related problems of individual and group living, present and future. It would orient education directly to present and future possibilities, but always in light of past experience. The idea here is that all peoples in all cultures at all times in history have had to cope, for better or worse, with the enduring concerns and changing problems of living.

What are enduring life concerns and related problems of living? They are the chief activity areas to which people give most of their time, energy, effort and worry throughout their lives. Specifically, what are some of these basic life concerns? Four of them have already been mentioned: sex and family, productive work, citizenship, and self-realization. Many others are identifiable. The particular items and their phraseology are not nearly as important as the use of this concerns approach to curriculum redesign. It is not desirable to absolutize some basic life concerns list and then defend it as being all-inclusive. Instead, a few possibilities will be considered and used as examples. These and others should be discussed at length, and additions or deletions should be made according to thorough sociological examination. For the purposes of this discussion, the following are identified as basic life concern activities:

Securing food and shelter
Protecting life and health
Communicating ideas and feelings
Adjusting to other people
Satisfying sexual desires
Enriching family living
Rearing children
Securing education
Sharing in citizenship
Controlling the environment
Utilizing leisure time
Enjoying beauty
Appreciating the past
Meeting religious needs
Finding personal identity
Adjusting to change
Growing old, facing death

Are not these some of the *enduring experiences of living* in which personal and community competence are essential and in which life's problems, small and large, are rooted? Are they not common to most cultures, places and times in history? Are they not the major life activities in which individuals, groups, societies and civilizations operate?

The Family of Man is a book reproducing a photographic exhibition assembled by Edward Steichen. In it are 503 pictures from 68 countries, picturing people in every cultural state from primitive to industrial. They portray lovers embracing, mothers with infants, children playing, people eating, working, dancing, grieving, consoling. Everything really important in human life seems basically the same — whether in jungles or cities, on farms or in slums, in all geographic areas of the world. The book's prologue by Carl Sandburg summarizes this commonality of humanity:[2]

> Alike and ever alike, we are on all continents in the need of love, food, clothing, work, speech, worship, sleep, games, dancing, fun. From tropics to arctics humanity lives with these needs so alike, so inexorably alike.

Just suppose that the required part of the curriculum consisted essentially of imaginative explorations into: 1) the ways through which people in one's own communities are now trying to deal with their major life concerns, tackling persistent problems both personal and group; 2) the reasons why they do as they do; 3) the ways people in different communities and varied cultures face the same issues; 4) the ways people in one's own and also in other communities and cultures did so at different periods of history; and 5) the ways people today might seek to develop more common goals and cooperative efforts for the greater good of all people in the future, despite differences in value systems.

To illustrate: People all through the ages, everywhere, have had to secure food if they were to survive. In primitive times and places they hunted animals for their food and later developed agriculture. With specialized labor came barter, then coinage, then further specialization and increased exchange. Now food is produced and distributed in many nations in highly industrialized fashion. Thus, the specific ways of getting food have varied from time to time and from culture to culture, but the fundamental life concern to secure food is ever the same. So it is with each of the other generic life activity experiences already noted.

Critical problems may arise whenever the goal-seeking activities prove inadequate, ineffective, exploitative or otherwise less than desirably successful. For example, the basic life concern to protect life and health includes, in all persons, communities, cultures and times, the problems of disease. If one is a member of a primitive tribe and gets sick, he may summon a medicine person to shake gourds, mutter incantations, and in such manner hope to drive away the evil spirit presumed to be causing the illness. An urban American, by contrast, will consult a physician for possible antibiotic medication. In short the specific procedures for dealing with life's problems differ in terms of place, time, and culture, but the basic life concerns remain the same.

Figure 5 contains examples of activities utilized to meet basic life concerns and includes some of the personal and group problems related to these life concerns.

If the core curriculum of the modern school and college were structured directly around systematic and sequential study through the years of such life-centered, human experiences, would that perhaps help young people and adults to develop a wider sense of identity with other humans who differ with them in ethnicity, living space, culture patterns, value systems, or historic eras? Might it help our whole human society surmount the

LIFE CONCERNS, ACTIVITIES, AND PROBLEMS		
AREAS OF CONCERN	A FEW DESCRIPTIVE ACTIVITIES	SOME RELATED PERSONAL AND GROUP PROBLEMS
Securing Food and Shelter	Hunting-manufacturing-pure food legislation-caves-condominiums-mortgages	Famine-malnutrition-fertilizers-slums-inflation
Protecting Life and Health	Police and fire protection-medical centers-Social Security	Diseases-mental illness-delinquency-crime
Communicating Ideas and Feelings	Reading-writing-languages-schools-art-music-mass media-sensitivity training	Illiteracy-stereotyped thinking-prejudices-paranoia
Adjusting to Other People	Warfare-slavery-unions-civil rights actions-marriage clinics	War-discrimination-delinquency-divorce
Satisfying Sexual Desires	Fantasy-masturbation-intercourse-celibacy	Venereal disease-sexual abuse-prostitution-pornography
Enriching Family Living	Marriage patterns-parent education-family services	Marital discord-child neglect-generational conflicts
Rearing Children	Varied family structure, patterns and practices	Sibling conflicts-discipline-child abuse
Securing Education	Family-schools-religious institutions-libraries-radio and television	Motivation-indoctrination-finances-ability differentiation
Sharing in Citizenship	Governments-political organizations-pressure groups-public opinion polls	Oppression-corruption-propaganda-apathy
Controlling the Environment	Fire building-bridges-dams-clothing-air conditioning	Floods-droughts-pollution-depletion of natural resources
Using Leisure Time	Games-sports-hobbies-music-dancing-reading-TV	Commercialization-lack of facilities-boredom
Enjoying Beauty	Architecture-graphic arts-music-outdoor living-gardens-nature areas	Sordid cities-pollution-environmental degradation-insensitivity
Appreciating the Past	Sagas-geneologies-artifacts-historical books-films	Ancestoral dominance-social stagnation
Meeting Religious Needs	Myths-rituals-centers of worship-instructional programs	Intolerance-fanaticism-religious wars
Finding Personal Identity	Puberty rites-slang language-hair, dress styles-youth organizations-finding self	Racism-sexism-parental domination-generational conflicts
Adjusting to Change	Future-oriented reading and TV viewing-status quo and progressive organizations-life span planning	Personal apathy-frustration-aggression-extremist politics
Growing Old, Facing Death	Youth lotions-hobbies-retirement planning-wills-religious consolation	Resentment-fears-poverty-euthenasia thinking-funeral wishes

Figure 5

ethnocentrism of nation, race, class, religion, age and sex, which continually thwarts our full development, sometimes threatens our welfare, and even menaces civilization? Could such a curriculum help bridge the generation gap as young people and adults together investigate, analyze and tackle some of the common problems of their community living? Could such studies and experiences relate school instruction closely with actual living and thereby make education more realistic and meaningful to more people? Might such a curriculum even help people develop emotional commitment, intellectual comprehension and the social skills necessary to build a new sense of humane common unity, without which the future of civilization on this planet is grim? Could this life-concerns approach, in brief, constitute the heart of living education for a needed new age in the history of humankind?

Alvin Toffler expressed support for this life-centered curriculum concept in a recent writing. In his view,

> The combination of action-learning with academic work, and both of these with a future orientation, creates a powerfully motivating and powerfully personal learning situation. It helps close the gap between change occurring "out there" and change occurring within the individual, so that learners no longer regard the world as divorced from themselves as immune to (and perhaps incapable of) change. In a turbulent, high-change environment, it is only through the development of "psychology of the future" that education can come to terms with learning.[3]

This is true, Toffler maintains, because:

> The world of the future will not be simply an oversized, overblown extension of the present envisioned by some futurists, but a world that will be dramatically different. It will be a world characterized by impermanence rather than by permanence; by rapid and accelerating change not only in our technology but in our values, in our sexual attitudes, in our relationships with family, friends, and organizations, and in the way we structure government, politics, and business.
>
> Similarly, the education system of the future will bear little resemblance to that of the present, even to the most innovative of today's educational experiments. There will be an entirely different approach to the curriculum, to the role and status of teachers, and to the process by which teachers are prepared for their careers. . . .
>
> One of the crucial things the schools must focus upon is values, but not in the traditional mode of inculcating a set of fixed, permanent values. Rather, the focus should include exploration of the value of values clarification.
>
> Much of what now happens inside the classroom should be moved out into the community. Students, working with adults, should be employed in a productive capacity to deal with community problems presently neglected. . . .

> The schoolhouse itself will change. Many of its current functions may be physically dispersed throughout the community. The concept that the classroom is the heartland of education will disappear. . . .[4]

QUESTION OF RELEVANCE

Education for better living is the central purpose sought. Yet this goal is obviously so vague as to be entirely useless unless it is sub-defined into myriad specific behavioral objectives. Unless that is done, this laudable purpose is about as meaningful as that proposed by a convention speaker who cheerfully announced that "the job of education is to take children from where they are to where they ought to be." True, but pointless.

Education for better living requires identification, pursuit and achievement of abilities to empathize with persons of other ages, races, religions and economic circumstances; to analyze political issues objectively; to purchase things wisely; to deal with children's fears creatively; to provide first aid skillfully; to prepare convincing job applications; to drive a car safely; and to attain a thousand other such important kinds of competencies. Each of these varied competencies relates directly to one or more of the major life concerns and can be planned for in function, scope and sequence in the new curriculum. Of course, the curriculum of general education must still be a structured one. But it must be organized around the basic life concerns of people, rather than as a continued presentation of the academic subject fields as such.

The term "relevance" is now so abused as to seem trivial. It is applied to everything from age groups to religion, not to mention education. Whole blocks of people, such as the old, or perhaps the middle-aged, or simply all those over thirty, have been relegated to the limbo of irrelevance. In politics the candidate who is dubbed irrelevant, or less relevant than another, will lose. And in the area of education, concern for relevance is even more pronounced, as it should be.

Neoprogressive educators often contend that relevancy must be a matter of individual definition, that it concerns the connections between a person's uniquely individual interests and various aspects of the total culture, and that therefore there can be no general curriculum content common for all students. In terms of socially minor concerns, the neoprogressives are correct, but *only* in such minor matters. Preferences for Chaucer, crayfish dissection, ping-pong, or pop music are obviously areas of purely personal relevancy. But the massive social menaces of environmental degradation, international war, racial and religious and class hatred, overpopulation, malnutrition, disease, and the like are incessantly relevant to all human beings, whether they realize it or not and regardless of what their immediate personal interests may be. In this larger sense, such basic human problems are inevitably relevant to each and to all and are thereby essential curriculum content for all.

But the deeper question is: *relevant to what?* To the momentary, fragmentary, often superficial interests of learners, as in so many of the old progressive and the new alternative schools? To the business of earning a living, as the current widespread career competence movement makes it? To the imperative task of building a worldwide society for the entire family of humankind? Or to what?

Perhaps all of the above are relevant in varying ways and with differing immediate and long-range goals. But, above all other considerations, today's education must be made meaningful in terms of modern youth's search for values in which to believe and to live by. Among young people there is a parched-ground hunger for significance in life — a deep yearning that is at its heart a spiritual quest. Even as they prepare themselves to seek entry into the economic world, growing numbers of youth feel deeply that the real satisfactions of life do not come through economic success. Yet all public school education is oriented toward just this goal. Where in American school education is there sustained and comprehensive concern for the significance of life in these tumultuous times?

In Asian cultures most education has always been related to the search for the meaning of life itself. All else is considered irrelevant. Without such personalized knowledge, it is believed, life is essentially unsatisfying, no matter how economically successful or immediately interesting it may be. It is no coincidence that in the West there is now a decided upswing in public interest in Eastern religion and philosophy, in devotion to gurus, and in the occult. Even fundamentalist Christianity is enjoying a surge of popularity among the young. These people are looking for *meaning*. Who am I? Why am I, I? What is life all about, really? American culture, and American education within it, has not been concerned about the fundamental questions of existence. Yet these questions are at the very heart of the problem of true relevance of education to living.

But even here the question of relevance cannot rest; it must be recognized that successful studies of the human condition require growing insight into history as well as imaginative gropings with the present and toward the future. This point has been well made by Sydney J. Harris, veteran syndicated newspaper columnist. He poses what is undeniably a central issue in curriculum planning today.*

> Young people are right in demanding that their studies be "relevant." What they don't understand, however, is relevant to "what." Nothing can be relevant to itself; the word needs a proper object.

---

*Reprinted by permission of Sydney J. Harris and Field Newspaper Syndicate.

> My 16 year old son informs me that many of his classmates have no interest in studying about Nazism and the causes and consequences of World War II. To them, the 1930's might as well be the 1630's; the past has no perspective for them; only the present has meaning.
>
> While professing "humanism," these young people are practicing barbarism. The barbarian doesn't care about the past, and therefore he feels free to violate the present. He is interested in a world of brute fact, not of values, and concentration on brute facts is the surest way to brutalize ourselves.
>
> Young people today think they care about values, and mean to. They are full of noble words like peace and love and cooperation and environment and justice — but they have no real idea of what these mean or how they can work out or why they failed to work out with previous generations who used the same noble words.
>
> But good intention built on ignorance is the surest way to turn idealism into cynicism; as the Romans knew, and said, the worst is a corruption of the best. . . .
>
> Unless we understand something of history, unless we have absorbed and analyzed the past, we cannot make rational judgments about the present — it is as futile as expecting a self-styled "doctor" to diagnose a patient without ever having studied medicine. No matter how much common sense, good will and natural aptitude he may have, he is not equipped to distinguish among ailments or prescribe for health.
>
> "Relevant" studies should mean relevant to the whole human condition, to man as a totality, in his work, his play, his love, his feelings, as much as of his economic and social arrangements. Relevance partakes of the past as much as it projects into the future; "what's past is prolong," said Shakespeare, in his truest line.[5]

Agreed. History, yes. *Relevant* history, imperatively! But not all history, even much history now commonly taught in school, is really relevant to intelligent civic decision-making in these unprecedented times. To say that "those who do not know history are condemned to repeat it" is merely to evade the implications of a vastly needed and very practical distinction: the distinction between what may be called *civic* history and *cultural* history.

Civic history is the story of fairly recent past events which bear quite directly upon the pressing problems and divisive issues of today and thereby provide needed perspective upon them; for example, slavery in America, President Wilson's fight for the League of Nations, Nazi Germany's racial philosophy, the atomic bombing of Hiroshima and Nagasaki, Watergate.

All other history is considered cultural. It is everything that is known to have happened but which is not directly influential upon us now: the Crusades, the War of 1812, covered wagons rolling westward, what Neil Armstrong said when he first stepped on the moon, and the like.

With this distinction, most of human history is cultural in nature; surprisingly little is civic. But that little is all-important!

Cultural history can be immensely interesting and, to those who find it so, intellectually and emotionally rewarding in high degree. For them the studies related to the Crusaders' cry "God Wills It!," our final psychological break away from English cultural dominance, the romance of the Oregon Trail and the immortal "One small step for a man, one giant leap for mankind" are all fascinating, and studies in such should be available on an elective basis. However, in the life-centered core curriculum to be experienced in varied ways by all students, *only civic history* should be required, and that always in terms of its directly discernible influence upon major problems which now or in the near future may confront the people. This distinction between civic and cultural history is obviously based upon *content* considerations. The *manner* of teaching may blur the difference. For example, an imaginative and socially committed educator might teach "covered wagons rolling westward" in such a way as to stimulate a futuristic pioneer attitude.

Systematic study of relevant civic history by each new generation is essential to the functioning of any democratic society, and probably to its continued survival as a democracy. Eric Sevareid, news commentator and analyst for the Columbia Broadcasting System and one of America's most distinguished political observers, knows this well. He pointed out that:

> Never in our history has there been such freedom of expression as there is today; never such concern with the downtrodden by the so-called Establishment; never such concern for youth; never such concern for defendants by police and court authority. Many who are young will take that as an astonishing statement. That is because youth can measure in only one direction — from things as they are, forward to their ideal of what things ought to be. They cannot measure backward, to things as they used to be, because they have not lived long enough; and they cannot measure laterally, to the condition of other societies on this earth, because they have not yet had the opportunity to know them well. Older people must add these two measurements. This is the core reason why the generation gap exists and why it will always exist.[6]

Always exist it will, in some measure, but action-centered community education can do a great deal to reduce that generation gap — *if* the core curriculum focuses upon the present and the future in light of the past and also expands its working concept of community from the local area outward to encompass the globe. But not otherwise.

So again the question: Relevance — to what? And again the essential answer: Relevance to the ongoing value struggles as well as to all of the basic domestic and international concerns and pressing problems of human living — through history, in these tumultuous times, and in the crucial years ahead as we must now try to envision them!

SOME PROBING QUERIES

What is the fundamental, ultimate reason for maintaining public schools and colleges in a democratic society? Surely that reason is threefold: to help transmit to each new generation the best of the human intellectual-aesthetic-ethical heritage; to help prepare individuals for personally satisfying, successful and creative living now and in the future; and to help provide society's educative basis for continuing social advance.

This triple and coordinative role of educational institutions is stressed because there probably are some critics who will claim that a life-concerns curriculum pattern is devoted to social reform rather than to education, that it will not prepare students in high school for college entrance, that it neglects the academic foundations required for further studies, that it is too utilitarian or too practical, that it is provincial and superficial in its essence, that it is just another kind of social studies program or, at any rate, a new set of subjects, that it is actually anti-intellectual in character, and that it constitutes preplanned programming which in that very fact is contrary to the true philosophy of community education.

It would be unwise to hastily overlook or dismiss these potential charges against a life-concerns curriculum. Therefore, each one is examined separately in the succeeding pages.

Social Reform Rather Than Education?

Nearly twenty-five years ago it was stated in the yearbook of the Association for Supervision and Curriculum Development that "In order to achieve the major purpose of today's schools — to improve community life — it is absolutely essential for school people to work with the community to use its resources and to serve the community through the educational program."[7]

What about that view? Is the major purpose of schools to improve community life? Is it not still to educate children and youth? Is a spurious purpose, community improvement, being substituted for the true one of educating children? Is this a genuine value dilemma, or is the apparent contradiction largely an artificial, semantic one? Is this a misunderstanding rooted deep in our common failure to understand how education actually occurs?

Clearly, it is the latter. Community educators who writhe under such criticism have only themselves to blame. Perhaps in their enthusiasm for more vital educational procedures, they have failed to think through the public relations image of the emerging community education philosophy. It is not what educators really mean that often disturbs the public and provides fuel for critics; it is rather what people think, or wish to think, they mean.

When educators talk about using the school to improve the community, they do so rightly and in all good faith. For as citizens and parents, as well as educators, they cannot be indifferent to the ways in which the community, and society, as a whole, actually educates. With Joseph K. Hart we must all become deeply aware that:

> No child can escape his community. He may not like his parents, or the neighbors, or the ways of the world. He may groan under the processes of living, and wish he were dead. But he goes on living, and he goes on living in the community. The life of the community flows about him, foul or pure: he swims in it, drinks it, goes to sleep in it, and wakes to the new day to find it still about him. He belongs to it: it nourishes him, or starves him, or poisons him; it gives him the substance of his life. And in the long run it takes its toll of him, and all he is.[8]

It *is* the function of community school education to improve the quality of living in the community, but it does so in order thereby to improve the quality of life education which that community is providing for all its people, consciously or not. Let it be clear among lay and professional people alike that the directing goal of educators is always that of better education of individuals. Their focus remains upon children, youth and adults as persons, as well as on community and societal improvement through education. While community educators demonstrate that community education is an immediate, positive force which the people themselves can use to solve their problems and better their living, they need also to show that this very process in itself provides the best education for everyone.

The life-concerns curriculum, if well designed and eagerly explored, concentrates on using the educational process to improve the quality of living in the individual life, as well as in that of the local, regional, and world communities. *Social reform is education* of the most vital, essential kind. And, conversely, functional education is the basis for democratic social reform.

Preparation for College Entrance?

The objection may be raised that regardless of superior learning values to be expected from such a life-concerns curriculum, it still cannot be accepted because it will not prepare students for conventional college entrance. They will lack the requisite academic subject credits which most colleges and universities still demand for entry.

The logical answer to that concern was given forty years ago. Beginning in 1933 the old Progressive Education Association conducted an objective and exciting "Eight Year Study" of that very problem. The progressives had largely abandoned the old conventional program of formal academic subjects in favor of serial units and learning projects organized about student interests. So they faced the same question that community education leaders who develop life-centered curricula must now confront: What about college entrance? To answer it, the P.E.A. persuaded some two hundred fifty colleges to admit recommended graduates of thirty selected progressive schools, even though those students lacked the required academic units. Some findings of this carefully designed and objectively evaluated "Eight Year Study" were impressive:

Graduates of the progressive schools were not handicapped in their college work;

Departures from prescribed patterns of academic subjects did not lessen students' readiness for the responsibilities of college study;

Students from schools which had made the most fundamental curricular revisions achieved in college distinctly higher standing than did students of equal ability with whom they were compared.[9]

Needed now is another "Eight Year Study," to be made as soon as warranted. This time it should evaluate results of a genuine community education approach in schools whose required curriculum centers in the enduring concerns and problems of living; *present* living (to discover needs), *past* living (for perspective and insight), and *future* living (to recognize options and plan for improvement). First, of course, genuine life-centered curricula will have to be developed in a number of dynamic community education centers. Second, arrangements will need to be made with several colleges and universities to accept students from such participating schools. That undoubtedly can be done, for colleges and universities these days are themselves in curricular flux and most of the institutions, especially those privately financed, are almost desperately seeking students. Many of them have already found, through evaluation of the "Upward Bound" and similar programs of recent years, that academic success in college is not necessarily dependent upon traditional subjects passed in high school. (The old belief dies hard, but it is going!).

How long shall secondary schools continue as professional slaves to conventional curricula, captives of the Carnegie unit system, content to push for mere evening and summer use of school buildings, development of citizens councils, and the like, yet leaving untouched, even unchallenged, the almost sacred patterns of traditional curricula? We need to venture forth to break with these old patterns and to devise new curricula that are truly meaningful in terms of real life needs today!

Neglect of Needed Academic Foundations?

Some may ask, how you can train future engineers if they do not study calculus in high school? And of course, that and similar questions can be asked for every kind of preprofessional and prevocational preparation. All such objections root in the old idea that these kinds of academically structured courses are foundational to precise technical achievement — which they are — and so are essential in the precollege curriculum — which they are not. Prospective engineers, physicians, journalists, salespeople, meter readers, auto mechanics and all such careerists need both life-concerns education and exacting technical training. The former should be central in their early years; the latter can start also as elective studies but for the most part be concentrated in the later high school, college and university years. At that time, with career choices essentially made and with greater maturity and increased motivation, students can and should plunge deeply and systematically into the requisite foundational disciplines required for their chosen fields of work.

Even in small schools, specific subject disciplines should be available and encouraged for those who desire them. Small group and independent studies can be arranged as part of students' elective programs. By all means, the few budding careerists in any field should be given what they need to know when they know that they want to master that field; but studies of what they do not need, will not need, and do not want should not be inflicted upon the uninterested students just because these studies will be needed by a few at a later time.

Too Utilitarian?

Some may feel that the life-concerns curriculum structure unduly emphasizes the practical problems of living, slighting or even totally ignoring the sheer enjoyment of intellectual and aesthetic pursuits. The art of the Aztecs, the sports of the Renaissance, the history of polar explorations and the like may excitingly interest some students. Can this proposed curriculum design meet those so-called impractical interests needs? If so, how?

Yes, it can, and it certainly should. Aztec art can well be included in the curriculum strand called Enjoying Beauty, Renaissance sports in Using Leisure Time, polar explorations in Appreciating the Past. In actual teaching, of course, almost every specific personal interest will overlap two or more of the suggested strand areas. Aztec art, for example, was more than beauty, it also communicated ideas and feelings and met religious needs. Any study of the sports of the Renaissance period might well include their relationships with other aspects of medieval life (Appreciating the Past) and some analysis of how sports related to the development of individual self-confidence then, in contrast to that process today (Personal Identity). Polar explorations clearly bear upon ways of Securing Food and Shelter, Protecting Life and Health under adverse physical conditions, Controlling the Environment as in the current Alaska oil fields development, enjoying Beauty such as that of the *aurora borealis* and of the midnight sun, and so on.

Utilitarian? What is more useful in happy living than fine, impractical studies that provide continued joy for those who find interest in them? Deep satisfactions for their own sakes are always important in happy living. They can and must have their honored place in the extended curriculum of community education.

Too Provincial?

Any school or larger educational institution that remains preoccupied with its own locality, or its own time in history, is indeed worthy of condemnation as being inexcusably provincial. Ours is a revolutionary era when we must think, feel, and plan in regional, national and worldwide terms, doing so with all the perspective that knowledge of past events and trends can provide. The curriculum must obviously be focused accordingly. Attention dare not be confined to the local community, here and now, interesting as that may be. We must accept not just local concerns, but also planetary worries!

Paul Hanna has usefully reminded us that:

> The word *community* is a generic term. To convey clear meaning this generic term should always be preceded by a modifier. We should speak or write about the *family* community, or the *neighborhood* community, or the *city* community, or the *metropolitan* community, or the *national* community, or the *Atlantic* community, or the *Inter-American* community, or the *Pacific* community, or the *world* community.[10]

The important transnational concept of community was vividly stressed by Henry Kissinger, United States Secretary of State, when he gave the keynote address to the first World Food Conference in Rome. Some 1200 delegates from 123 countries heard that speech which *Time* characterized as "probably signaling the start of a new era of international cooperation." *Time* introduced that story by reporting that during the "first seven days of talks . . . another 10,000 lives were lost to famine in Africa, Asia and Latin America. In the same period, another 1.4 million children were born into a world that already contains nearly half a billion starving people." Kissinger said, in part, that:

> We are faced not just with the problem of food but with the accelerating momentum of our interdependence. We are stranded between old conceptions of political conduct and a wholly new environment, between the inadequacy of the nation-state and the emerging imperative of global community. The contemporary agenda of energy, food and inflation exceeds the capacity of any single government, or even of a few governments together, to resolve.[11]

Obviously the local geographic and ethnic communities are the locales in which much firsthand educational experiencing can be arranged and conducted. But the local community is never self-sufficient economically, politically or educationally. Therefore, "community" can best be conceived as a series of interlocking concentric circles: local, regional, national, planetary, often cross-hatched by ethnic and other culture dimensions.

Is the Curriculum Superficial?

Most of us recognize that in every community, whatever its area or time, there exists three kinds of interrelated levels of culture which must be comprehended and worked with: the material, the institutional, and the psychological. *

> *Material level.* This is the external civilization, the *things* people use or have made, as well as the people themselves. It includes a community's natural resources; the means by which it produces and distributes goods and services; the physical setting of the community — housing, streets, transportation system; its parks and playgrounds; water supply and sanitation service; communication facilities; protective services; its coal mines, bee hives, lakes, fire engines, housing projects, and the like . . . .
> *Institutional level.* Here are the organized or institutionalized ways of living, the *mass habits* of the people. This second level is less tangible, but extremely significant in determining the community's behavior; it is the "cradle of custom" into which each child is born. Marriage customs, family form, governmental practices, religious rituals, the language used, number system followed, the common arrangements for economic exchange and monetary usage, all illustrate the institutional level of the culture . . . .
> *Psychological level.* Determining the customs and the material creations of the community are the motivations of the people. These are the desires that produce activity; the fears which inhibit behavior; the attitudes which pattern acceptable conduct; the values, goals, ideals, loyalties, and taboos which influence and direct human behavior. . . .[12]

Increasingly, even the outer geographic circle areas are also resources for valuable firsthand experiencing through field studies as well as audio-visual representations. So also are the three cultural levels within all community areas. Since even local areas are microcosms of larger communities, it is important to remember that understanding of the cultural levels and the life concerns within the local community can provide the necessary conceptual basis for comprehending other local and larger areas in both time and space. Genuine community studies are never superficial.

Just Another Social Studies Pattern?

What is here proposed, some may assert, is really only another format for a social studies curriculum. This seems a plausible observation in terms of the traditional separation of disciplines and the catch-all nature of the social studies. It is true that the life-concerns structure here suggested does center in human group interrelationships with people and with the physical and cultural environment, but it actually goes far beyond even the broadest

*From *School and Community* by Edward G. Olsen and others. Prentice-Hall, Inc., 1954, pp. 81-82. Used by permission.

present social studies patterns. For example, it should include in-depth studies of atoms and galaxies, but always in direct relation to one or more of the life-concern areas, not as parts of a science course organized as such. It will require extensive reading in English literature, not as an isolated survey of that subject, but within the immediate contexts of the several concerns fields. This same relationship occurs for much of the content of the conventional disciplines.

Children must be taught to read, better than they are now! Since they learn to read by reading, they should read stories of social significance from their earliest years. Fifth grade readers, to illustrate, might well include anthropological accounts emphasizing the similarities as well as the differences in life styles of children around the world.

The required life-concerns curriculum, in brief, should be a sequential and expanding exploration of relevant aspects of literature, science, art, music, dance, mathematics, homemaking, civics and all others of the traditional subjects. However, these elements should always be taught in direct and immediate relation to the life concerns under study, not as isolated discipline subjects in themselves.

Is the Curriculum Too Structured?

An often-raised criticism of the conventional academic subject structure is that it is too prepackaged; its content, at least, is chosen and organized by professional curriculum designers and teachers rather than by the students themselves. Such prepackaging, it is alleged, does not meet students' individual interests, thus lacks motivational appeal, and therefore is not acceptable in the modern school. Alternative school supporters usually make much of this charge and so encourage students to design their own curricula as they see fit.

This same objection may be raised against the proposed life-concerns plan, that it, too, is prestructured into essential areas and so can eventuate in an equally rigid curricular structure. Critics might ask: Is not the student-chosen project the only valid alternative to any planned curriculum, whether traditional or life-centered?

Yes, the curriculum here proposed is structured into several fundamental areas of human experience here called life concerns. But, within each of those broad areas, there is vast room and plentiful opportunity for cooperative student planning and individualization. From early ages and continuing with ever wider scope, children and youth should be involved in deciding and developing their own specific learning activities. The life-concerns curriculum is as broad as life itself; that is precisely why this approach is inherently far more flexible and therefore individually more functional than the academic subject structure can ever be.

No, the unrelated project pattern is not an acceptable alternative. Student interests are splendid springboards for motivation, but they are often shallow, superficial, and seldom comprehensive. No society, and especially a democratic one, can maintain its institutional strength and stability if it leaves curriculum content choice to what are often the ephemeral whims of immature youngsters. That is why it is supreme folly for education and community leaders to continue to ignore the most imperative issue in education today: *What should youth and adults learn through the school curriculum? What shall we teach to assure those essential learnings? How shall the curriculum be structured?*

If people hope to cope with life today and somehow build a better tomorrow, then surely they must have much guided, successful experience in dealing with their own life concerns in their own immediate and wider communities. They must be systematically helped to comprehend their world of today and its possibilities for the future, not piecemeal, not sporadically, not erratically, but as a vast web of interrelated social processes and resultant problems which have changed through times past, which constitute our societal matrix of today, and which project for us alternative options for the future. Without some such fundamental curriculum structure, organized education is bound to be chaotic, frequently futile, sometimes negative in its effects, and largely frustrating to most students and teachers alike.

Anti-Intellectual in Character?

The community schools and colleges that provide services to the adult community may be doing so with high success. Yet, in their regular instructional programs, they may not be amply educating the students. Learning of functionally irrelevant material is not true education. Neither is mere learning activity. Learning about recognized problem-needs by thoughtfully doing something is required. Certainly students may begin with real-life needs as evident in local situations, but unless they analytically go from them backward and forward in time, and outward around the world, they will neither develop essential social perspective nor arrive at valid principles to assist them in facing future situations. A curriculum that does not intellectualize its community studies and service projects in terms of humankind's basic processes and problems of living should indeed be charged with anti-intellectualism, however sincere its intentions or how well-accepted its program.

In this critical period of history it is imperative to make clear that the democratic schools's goal is always the better education of individuals. We had better keep our accent on children and youth as well as upon the community problem-solving function of community education. While educators demonstrate that community education is an immediate, positive force which the people themselves can use to improve the quality of living, let them also show that this very process in itself can provide the best kind of helpful education in the regular school day.

How should the charge that the life-concerns curriculum is actually or potentially anti-intellectual in its basic character be evaluated? Is that charge true, or is the life-concerns curriculum, on the contrary, an educational approach that requires of its students the utmost in disciplined thinking, creative imagination, and working familiarity with the best of human experience and projected possibilities?

Perhaps an illustration will show how the life-concerns curriculum emphasizes hard intellectual grappling with the origins, causes, status, effects and suggested treatment of a persistent and serious community and personal problem. The example will be that of Preserving Mental Health.

Suppose that the members of a high school or community college class would like to see what might be done to improve mental health in their own lives and in their local community. What are the types of information, understandings, concerns, attitudes and skills these people would need to investigate in order to study and research such a project? They would have to ferret out and evaluate objectively such factors as the community life conditions that contribute to emotional tensions; the rates and status of juvenile delinquency, divorce, alcoholism and drug use; ethnic and religious and social-class tensions. Other factors for their consideration could include past and present theories of causes of mental illness; local counseling agencies and clinics; psychiatric services, mental hospitals, human relations organizations, mental health associations; school guidance programs and their effectiveness; comparisons of present treatment of the mentally disturbed in the United States with that of past times and also with that in other countries now; the broad religious and ethical values underlying our concern for the improvement of human welfare; and the principles of good mental hygiene which one should try to embody in his or her own life values and living style.

There need be no soft pedagogy whatever in such a learning project in the life-concerns-centered curriculum!

Can such life-related study projects really improve community treatment of the mentally ill? In further illustration, these class participants plus cooperating citizens and local organizations, might conclude that a family welfare agency is needed in their town and should be established. They could therefore together devise a plan with all its manifold details, present and publicize that plan throughout the community, and then help get out to vote if the matter had to come before the electorate. Meanwhile, these people would be learning how to go about affecting local community change within the governmental system. Even if they lost the election that very experience could teach them much about local politics. Meanwhile, they would have been learning intellectually and specifically how to deal better with their own emotions, to be more mature in their own judgments, and, hopefully, how to be better citizens in the years ahead.

Does all this sound anti-intellectual? Or is it the very source of disciplined and creative thinking at its best? Throughout the entire learning process the life-concerns curriculum approach should emphasize depth of understanding, critical analysis, historical perspective, transcendance of past experience, problem-solving, inventing the future, seeking sound policies and programs to implement it, and comprehending power and decision-making processes. Are not these all intellectual qualities of the highest caliber and worth?[13]

Static Program Rather Than Dynamic Process?

In some quarters it is almost routine to assert that community education is properly a process, not a program. That alliterative slogan — "process, not progam" — is admirable, within limits. Certainly community education is a cooperative planning process. It is not a unilateral, manipulative procedure toward some predetermined blueprinted program sought by a few. Of course, community education must develop creative input from many sources within the community as well as from the educators themselves. Widespread and continuing community involvement must be the process by which the basic curriculum program is decided. But there is real danger in the "process, not program" formula, the subtle hazard that educators may come to feel that genuine community education is being developed just because some community members are actively involved in school-centered programs and are helping to plan wider educational activities.

However much community involvement in planning emerges, that process may still leave the institution's conventional purposes and regular curriculum untouched, unaffected, unchanged. "Process, not program" can easily rationalize complacency about the essential character of the traditional curricular program of studies which so drastically fails to meet the real educational needs of most children, youths and adults today.

What is to be done? Must not process produce functional programming? Unless community involvement results in community and institutional awareness of the critical curricular problems it will fail, however active and continuous that citizen involvement may become. Educators have come a long way, yes; but the conventional curricular problem still confronts all planners and now demands their imaginative and creative thinking within the planning process. A totally new and functionally effective curriculum pattern must be cooperatively designed and developed. Instead of trying rather futilely to maintain the old or to add some minor improvements to it, communities should begin to experiment (even in small ways and with slow beginnings) toward cumulative development of a life-concerns curricular structure. Let everyone, educators and community people together, develop better education through a more realistic and effective curriculum, cooperatively designed.

We must go even beyond the idea that school curriculum should be structured around the major concerns, processes, and problems of life rather than around the traditional subjects of study. We must go forward with the philosophy succinctly expressed by Maurice F. Seay when he wrote, "I would insist that the people of every community need a living-centered curriculum in a community-wide educational program composed of the coordinated programs of all educational agencies."[14]

The need to move beyond community school into community education was well stated by Clyde Campbell in a noteworthy overview of the community school movement. He insightfully contrasted the typical community school programs of the 1930s with the far wider social needs of today. He pointed out that those pioneer community school programs were typically small town or local neighborhood improvement activities such as raising chickens, planting trees, building recreation halls or getting out the vote. But then, assessing the temper of today, Campbell concluded that:

> All this was noble — practical — highly educative — it furthered a spirit of cooperative living that might well be emulated in any period of history. In truth, such a description of brotherly living tends to lead one, even now, into a state of sweet sublimity. And I am told that citizens of this generation did, on occasion, have feelings of eternal bliss because people were sharing, caring, sacrificing and doing things for each other. Yes indeed, I am convinced that it is the way all of us should strive to live in neighborhoods today. "What is life all about if it isn't to make the world better for each other?" That is a fair question to ask. But reluctantly, I must return to the temper of *our* times. I really cannot see this program, alone, solving the social conflicts of the seventies. As a process, I doubt that it can come to a tight grip with wars, crime, air pollution, water pollution, political corruption, violence in the streets and what not. Surely a more comprehensive kind of community education is needed in the decades to come.[15]

Yes, Campbell is so right! That is why community education in our time cannot succeed unless its central outlook is broadened, updated. That philosophy must have a newer, wider thrust. And it must permeate the schools and other educational agencies throughout entire areas, not be confined to the smaller political units of cities, suburbs, and school districts.

In a recent book Seay mentioned three obligations of the community school within the community education process:

> To influence the existing programs of all educational agencies to the end that they are more and more based upon the community education concept that community education achieves a balance and a use of all institutional forces in the education of all the people of a community;

To provide the means for cooperative planning, coordinating, and evaluating;

To add to programs of established agencies or to a cooperative operational plan involving two or more agencies those educational activities determined to be needed to fill gaps so that a balanced program is available for all people of a community.[16]

The life-centered curriculum must not be considered as a static program but rather must be developed through a dynamic process.[16]

"School Ladder" Is Suggested?

If the proposed curriculum patterning is to be of maximum learning value to students, it must be made central in the school experience from early years upward. Figure 6 delineates how centrality in life concerns could be developed within the traditional school structure, including college, university and post-graduate levels. The chart is obviously much oversimplified; necessarily so. However, a few explanations of its salient features may be helpful.

The plan is designed for lifelong learning, beginning with nursery school, moving through the twelfth grade and on into community college, four-year college, university, and/or on into continuing adult learning.

In early years, emphasis is placed upon socialization and communication abilities, but even then introduces the child to the concept of life concerns.

The life concerns areas are "discovered" as realities within the personal experience of every child. In those years major attention is given to mastery of the 3 R's, development of multiculture empathy, and growth in group skills — all within the framework of various life-concerns processes as these operate in the immediate geographic communities and on the material and institutional levels of culture. (See page 120.)

During the adolescent years, when minds reach mental maturity, the life-concerns explorations are continued in more depth and additional dimensions. Furthermore, the personal and social problems which appear in the life-concerns areas are studied, with special immersion in the sociological sea of conflicting views and values — the motivational level of culture.

Most K-12 students will normally continue (perhaps after a work, travel or leisure "stay-out") into and through the community college level. Here they will pursue self-chosen career and other personal interests.

Those who wish may later transfer into a standard college or university for further training and degrees. Perhaps a few highly gifted and early choice professional careerists may be accepted directly into a university where the advancement of knowledge, professional competence, and

PROPOSED SCHOOL LADDER:
STRUCTURE & CORE CURRICULUM

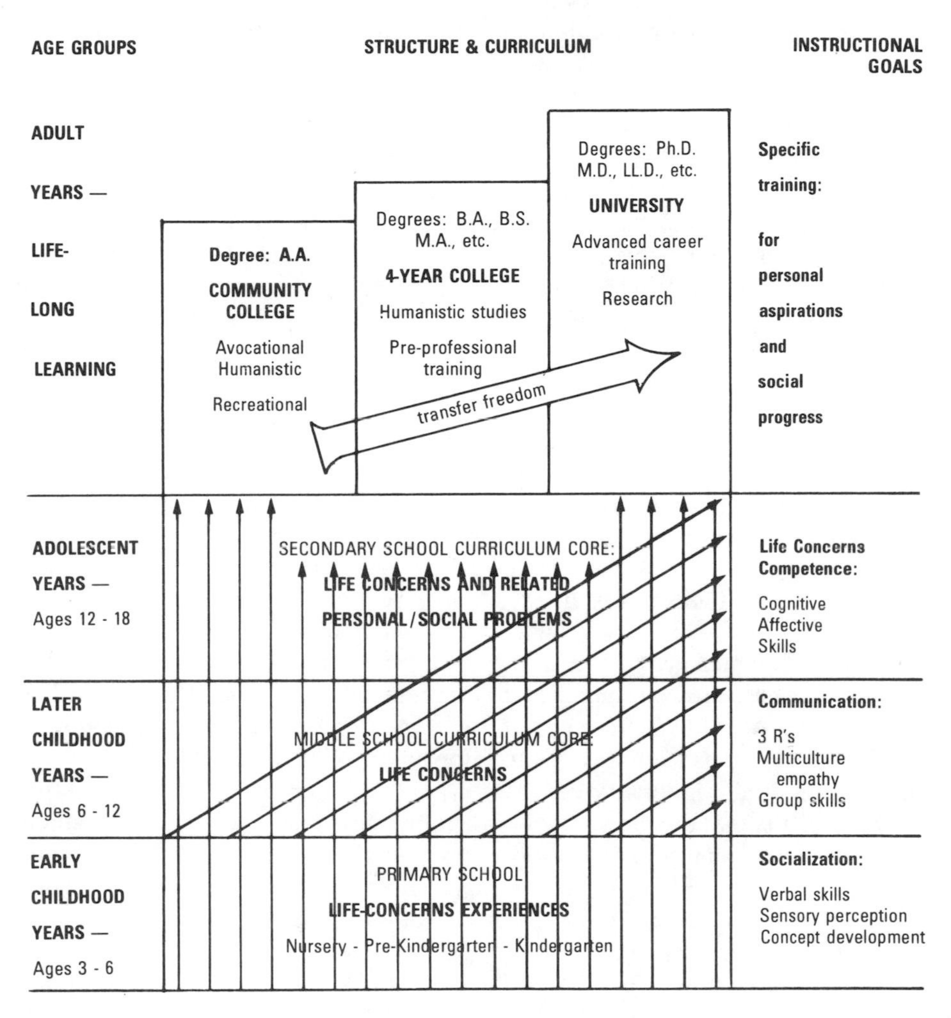

Figure 6

further degrees are primary goals. There should be relatively easy transfer possibility from any one adult program to any other.

Many adults will want to pursue systematically or otherwise their own interests, regardless of degree programs. Full encouragement should be given them, and equal opportunity, regardless of their previously attained or unattained academic levels.

The life-concerns curriculum should predominate during the childhood and adolescent years, but with all possible opportunity for the gifted and the already-decided-special-interest boys and girls to elect systematic study of academic and other discipline areas also.

The conventional discipline subjects should predominate in the adult years, but with all possible opportunity for men and women to elect informal studies of their own choosing.

Those parameters, then, define the basics of an educational ladder — full, free, and functional! Such a structure is a major dimension of community education, still largely ignored, but now imperatively important!

LIBERAL EDUCATION

Some people may assert that community education and the life-concerns curriculum threaten liberal education. Such critics should remember that true liberal education is that which liberates people from blind subservience to the mores of their groups as these have been defined by the accidents of having been born into a particular group, place, and period of history. Liberal education means a freeing of the mind from provincial pettiness in every field. It is perspective at its best. It is to "see life steadily and see it whole" as Matthew Arnold wisely noted. *To see life steadily and to see it whole* — and then take constructive steps to improve it, is the heart and the purpose of life-centered community education.

This means that the curriculum of the democratic school must be designed to help people comprehend themselves and their societies in all relevant dimensions — historic, contemporary, futurist — and in psychological, sociological, scientific, literary, artistic, religious, political, economic and philosophic terms as well.

There is even more than that to the educational viewpoint here proposed. The intellect does not operate in an emotional vacuum. Almost above all else, youth today need a sense of *belonging,* of *being wanted* by society in times of peace as well as as during years of crisis. If only for psychological maturation and emotional stability, each boy and girl must develop a personal conception of *individual worth* through achievement of *social recognition.* Somehow we must find ways to give *all* our children and young people a realistic understanding of their world and extensive opportunity to participate with satisfactions and recognition in its basic processes of living. Then they may develop feelings of true achievement, personal worth, and social sensitivity which are essential to emotional adjustment and to active democratic citizenship. If we cannot, then there is grave danger that the new adults of the 1980s and beyond, disillusioned with the social unreality of the traditional schools and colleges, may express their accumulated frustration through native fascist movements destructive of democracy itself.

The world of tomorrow holds much promise as well as real hazard for youth and for education. If we can succeed in creating educational experiences which are psychologically satisfying and socially creative, and which function that way in all teaching areas at all school levels, we may expect to witness during the remainder of this century a vital expansion of democratically effective living, both personal and societal, at home and even worldwide. But this requires that we speedily relate education to life experience, school instruction to individual and community needs, and teaching and learning to living at its highest and best.

In the light of pressing social realities, it is not enough to say that the role of education is to "help each person develop to his or her maximum potential." That is true, but not enough! Surely we must go beyond this platitude to help people comprehend human behavior through the ages, to understand better that of today, to appreciate and strengthen the values and ethical aspirations of both democracy and the brotherhood idea, and to develop curricular programs incorporating these values and their implied educational goals. What and how all this is to be done at the individual school centers and in different community circumstances is a matter for continuous planning, experimentation and evaluation.

Can we do it? How may we find and educate the school and community leaders to make it possible? These are some of the questions the authors ask readers to consider in the next chapter.

6. LEADERSHIP FOR CURRICULUM CHANGE

A major implication of the community education concept is that the public school system is one of many contributing forces in the education of the people. The role of the school is not diminished except by the need for cooperative action when it recognizes the fact that there are many educational agencies in every community that have legitimate educational aims — and that each agency has a right to serve and be served.

Now, in a period of resource scarcity and criticism of waste, the possible contributions of all forces in the education of the people are more readily appreciated and accepted. Yes, the school is tremendously important, and because of its great resources of human talent and physical facilities, is most often the catalytic agent which takes the leadership role in establishing the organizational and administrative structure necessary for community-wide planning and coordination. The school is also the agency which is more likely to offer the educational services needed to provide adjustments . . . in the 'balance' of community-wide educational resources.

— Maurice F. Seay, *Community Education: A Developing Concept*

It is evident from a look at the enormous gap between our collective human needs and the nature and scope of learning experiences provided by educational institutions of our society that major changes are necessary. These changes should not be made in an unplanned fashion nor effected just for the sake of change; they should create procedures to provide those learning experiences which can best improve the quality of living for every individual and the entire community. To assist individuals of all ages and backgrounds to have more productive, healthy and enjoyable lives should be the ultimate goal of any educational institution. This goal can best be accomplished when these institutions, be they elementary or secondary schools, community colleges or universities, operate from the needs levels of their clients.

If one accepts this basic philosophy, then the need for fundamental change within these educational systems can be recognized.

ABOUT CHANGE

Much has been written and spoken about change. Yet, it appears an unsophisticated science. Even less is really known about institutional change. It does seem evident that institutions do not change until basic values and attitudes of their leaders and consumers are modified. Very often, institutions are criticized as if they were living beings, but *they* do not think or act. Institutional behavior is the direct result of beliefs held by people associated with the institution, and most of these beliefs relate directly to the past experiences of the people involved. As individuals, our actions, reactions, and interactions are based primarily on our life experiences. We are, so to speak, our experiences.

Educational institutions themselves, status roles within the institutions, and people in general are often sighted as the blockers or restrictors to significant change. These are not the *real* foes. The real foes are less tangible. They include people's values and attitudes, desires to maintain tradition, and "tunnel vision." People's behaviors are based on their attitudes, which emanate from their systems of values. What and how people think about something relates directly to their ordering or prioritizing of values, characterized by such words as altruism, honesty, knowledge, loyalty, pleasure, power and wealth. An example of such prioritizing occurred during the Watergate break-in and coverup of the early 1970s. Each of the participants in this event had to make decisions between honesty-loyalty, loyalty-power, and so forth. Obviously, people do not consciously prioritize such value characteristics but do unconsciously behave according to their beliefs or attitudes which are based on their systems of values. From what do values emanate? Values evolve from the past experiences of the individual. Life experiences of an individual, regardless of age, reflect his or her system of values. The evolution-of-behaviors model shown in Figure 7 illustrates this relationship.

Simply stated, the most effective way to change people's actions is to modify their attitudes and beliefs by providing relevant and emotionally satisfying new experiences. These can include status, prestige and privileges as well as financial rewards. Many attempts to force or coerce people into

EVOLUTION OF BEHAVIORS

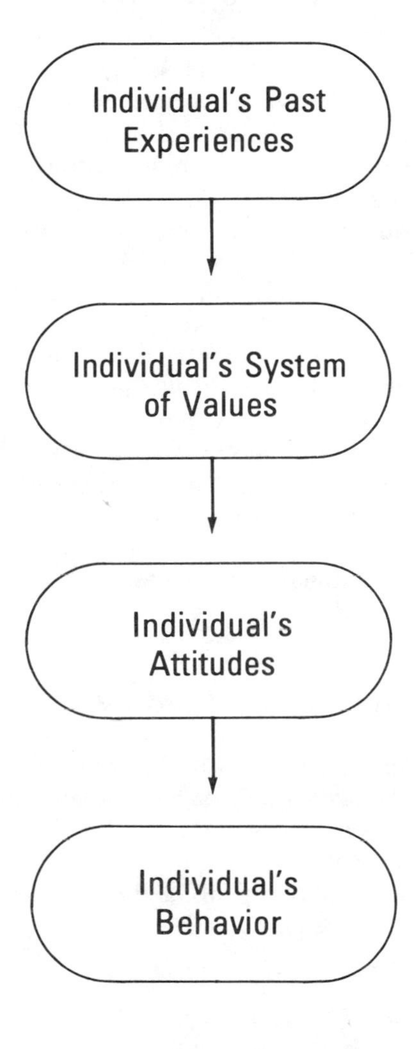

Figure 7

behavioral change have been relatively ineffective, because the people involved were not believers in the desired change. Successful change will occur only when those involved have developed emotional commitment to the change.

Recognizing this fact, it is clear that the most effective way to bring about systematic educational change is to expose the individuals involved to new experiences. Care must be taken, however, to make sure these experiences are good ones and that they are presented in a slow-sell manner, allowing for assimilation, questioning, thinking, and synthesis. Too often, good ideas have been hard sold, only to have them rejected or not received because of the approach itself. Emphasis should be placed on providing direct learning opportunities, allowing for exploration, examination, discussion, and application to the participants' situations. Visitation of ongoing demonstrations and internships are two very effective means for delivering a soft-sell approach.

The amiable cartoon character named Pogo stated: "We have met the enemy, and he is us." The enemy to educational change is not we as people, but rather the attitudes and values we hold. Since our values result from our experiences, it is essential that we attack the problem at that level. Obviously, this kind of approach will take much leadership and a considerable amount of time. However, it is the best approach. The school system we have today has evolved through many decades. Obviously, much effort and time will be needed to reconstruct its formal curriculum.

Leadership is necessary in all educational endeavors but is particularly important in constructive educational change.

NECESSARY LEADERSHIP

Discussions about leadership styles and techniques usually conclude that most approaches can be successful, depending upon the situation and the individuals involved. Effective community education, however, requires a particular leadership approach.

Leadership approaches may be divided into two general categories: leader-centered, and other-centered.

Leader-Centered

Leader-centered leadership is a behavior wherein the goals, direction and creative thinking are vested in the leader rather than in the people. The approach is epitomized by the "Joan of Arc" leader who rallies people around a common banner and directs them toward the tasks, much like Joan led her troops. This general approach is obviously effective in particular situations, but it is far over-utilized in educational leadership. Its extensive use has restricted emergent leadership from within the group.

The leader-centered style is essentially a follow-me approach with definite leader-follower roles. Thus, the major role of the leader is to gain from the follower increasing support toward his or her preconceived goals and increasing service in the achievement of these goals. Emergent leadership by the people is not encouraged. The probable reason for extensive use of the leader-centered approach is that it is an easier form of leadership because fewer people are involved in direction-setting and the leader does not have to confront group diversity head on. It is also an expedient means of achieving the leader's own goals.

Programs and endeavors resulting from this type of leadership often continue to exist only as long as a strong leader remains in control. Many times, however, productivity begins to decrease when the leader leaves. In the case of preconceived goals, dependency on the leader probably is more expedient, but, unfortunately, does not encourage continuity. The real test of leadership is the degree to which there is continued growth and achievement after the leader has left the scene.

A second weakness of the leader-centered approach is that a project is perceived as the leader's own program, rather than as that of the organization or group. The personality of the leader becomes very important, simply because people may offer resistance or not contribute to programs or endeavors that provide increased credit to the leader or in which the leader is perceived to project a negative image. Many good educational endeavors have not been evaluated objectively on their own merits, but have instead been judged by their advocates. Every attempt must be made to allow proposals to stand and be judged objectively, apart from their advocates or protagonists. One of the most effective ways to accomplish this is to refrain from a leader-centered approach and to invest leadership in the entire group.

Other-Centered

The facilitative leader approach was aptly described in 565 B.C. by Lao-Tse:

> A leader is best
> When people barely know he exists.
> Not so good when people obey and acclaim him,
> Worse when they despise him.
> "Fail to honor people,
> They fail to honor you";
> But of a good leader, who talks little,
> When his work is done, his aim fulfilled,
> They will say, "We did this ourselves."[1]

This other-centered approach vests leadership in others rather than in status leaders. Leaders using this approach make it possible for others to emerge and assume responsibilities. They help people become as involved in task development and completion as they wish to be involved and encourage them to apply their skills and creative thinking to mutually determined goals.

There are several advantages to utilizing a facilitative leadership approach. First, it allows for continuity of operation, since leadership is not vested in any one person. The leadership is not only shared by many, it is also situational. All participants have the opportunity and are encouraged to provide emergent leadership in different situations.

A second advantage of facilitative leadership is that such leaders recognize that all people possess different values and beliefs and help the group capitalize on this diversity. Members have the opportunity to interpret each situation in their own way and yet advocate a common endeavor. The entire group benefits from diversity of individual members when the goals, direction, and creative thinking are vested in many people.

Another advantage of facilitative leadership is that it encourages objectivity in program evaluation. As previously mentioned, the leader-centered approach often causes people to perceive the endeavor as the leader's program, thus allowing the personality of the leader to affect their judgment of the program's worth. The charismatic leader could perpetuate the continuation of a weak program, where a strong program could be panned or blocked because of a dislike for the leader. Facilitative leadership allows for greater objectivity because it disperses program ownership in many people and minimizes the influence one person might have on the relative worth of a program.

A fourth advantage relates directly to the term "synergism," which was described in Chapter Four. The effects of shared leadership do have the potential to exceed the sum of effects generated by individual members with one status leader. Great athletic teams have nearly always had several members who emerge at different times and situations to assume leadership of the team. Shared leadership allows for the highs and lows all individuals experience in mood and productivity.

Although the facilitative approach has advantages over that which is leader-centered, it is more difficult to achieve. The leader-centered approach is initially easier because it vests the goals, direction, and creative thinking in the status leader, which obviously allows for more control. But facilitative leadership is more effective in the final outcome because it insures continuity and utilizes the diversities found among the group members.

What are the characteristics of a facilitative leader? Is such leadership inborn or can it be acquired? Where might the leader secure more information on facilitative leadership?

A recent publication by Joseph Wittmer and Robert D. Myrick is probably the best source of information on facilitative leadership, even though it was written primarily for the classroom teacher.[2] Wittmer and Myrick identify six major characteristics of a facilitative teacher. These are the same for a good facilitative leader. The following descriptions — effective listening, genuineness, understanding, respect, intelligence, skill in interpersonal communication — were selected from Wittmer and Myrick's discussion on characteristics of the facilitative teacher. *

> *Effective Listening* — Listening can . . . improve hearing deeper levels of communication. That is, a good listener not only attends to all the literal meanings, he also makes a special effort to understand the personal meaning of a speaker's words.
>
> The listener who wants to become a facilitator hears the words and responds to the ideas that are communicated by focusing on the personal meaning that accompanies the spoken word.
>
> *Genuineness* — Genuineness implies authenticity. It means not playing a role. It denotes being in tune with yourself and acting in a way that reveals self congruence. It is extremely difficult to feel one thing and communicate the opposite.
>
> When one assumes a role that is not characteristic of his total self, his ability to positively facilitate others will decline, and he may not be helpful at all.
>
> *Understanding* — Being genuine is important; however, it does not mean necessarily that one will understand another. As we genuinely listen and discover a student's (person's) perceptions, we begin to respect and understand him.
>
> Empathy means understanding another person, especially what he is feeling . . . , Empathy means coming to know, to value, and to respect another person from his frame of reference rather than ours. When you have empathetic understanding . . . you have an awareness of his internal frame of reference without approving or disapproving it and without losing your own frame of reference.
>
> *Respect* — Respect for an individual means accepting his experiences as an important part of him. In other words, respect his feelings unconditionally. We accept him as a person with the human potential for joys, depressions, successes, and failures . . . . This encourages us to search for the individual rather than approving or disapproving of his thoughts or behaviors.
>
> Respect goes beyond optimism or simple reassurance. It is the communication of deep interest and concern. A high positive regard . . . emphasis that his personal dignity is valued, his personal feelings are accepted, and that he is not being judged.

*From *Facilitative Teaching: Theory and Practice,* by Joe Wittmer and Robert D. Myrick, (pp. 42-48). Copyright © 1974 by Goodyear Publishing Co. Reprinted by permission.

Intelligence — At times, a knowledgeable person (leader) can expedite the learning process by presenting his experiences and ideas. At other times, he will want to help students (people) to become more knowledgeable through their own experiences and will serve as simply a catalyst in the learning situation.
(Note: To this description, the authors of this volume would add the need for the leader to be knowledgeable in group leadership techniques, individual behavior in groups, and evolution of a collegial group.)
Skill in Interpersonal Communication — Much of what society is and much of what it will become is an outcome of our effectiveness in establishing interpersonal relationships. People are a vital part of our lives. We need others in order to be fulfilled as a person, to experience all of our human potentiality. When our relationships are positive and open, we can experience all of our humanness. We can move toward personal fulfillment. We learn and help others to learn. We feel alive and enjoy life. On the other hand, when our relationships lack personal involvement, or when they restrict our personal growth, then we feel an inhumanness that is reflected in a joyless kind of existence. The facilitative teacher (leader) knows that effective interpersonal communication skills are needed if a student (person) is to be positively assisted in his drive for self enhancement. Moreover, the facilitative teacher (leader) knows that effective interpersonal skills do not just happen by chance; they are learned.
The facilitative teacher (leader) is sensitive to the impact of words on individuals. He is interested in a language of feelings as well as ideas. He knows that although nonverbal communication plays an important part in our relationships, verbal communication is the critical factor in the learning process. He knows that our words reflect our attitudes and feelings as much as our ideas do. A few carefully chosen words can communicate an invitation to talk, to risk, to come closer. Whereas, ill chosen words push people away, close communication, threaten relationships, and impede learning.[2]

These, then, are the major characteristics of a facilitative leader. All six are learnable skills. Continuous self-evaluation on the part of the leader is important; one must continuously question how he or she is doing in respect to each of these categories. But self-evaluation alone is not sufficient. Specific training in facilitative leadership is imperative. Two of the most complete sources of information on facilitative leadership techniques are the *Handbooks of Structured Experiences for Human Relations Training* and the *Annual Handbooks for Group Facilitators*, edited by J. William Pfeiffer and John E. Jones.[3] With a combination of these tools, interpersonal skills, and management competencies, the community educator can become an effective facilitative leader.

The facilitative leader must not only have interpersonal skills, but also possess the four management skills of diagnosis, prescription, treatment, and evaluation. It is necessary to note that these skills are not separate entities, but rather comprise a dynamic sequential approach to effective facilitative leadership. Although each skill can be acquired and used separately, it is essential for the facilitative leadership to utilize these elements as a concise format, rather than relying on a random or trial-and-error method of implementing change. Through the use of such a process, the facilitative leader can develop self-renewing, self-correcting groups of people who learn to organize themselves according to the nature of the tasks at hand.

How might one utilize the identified management skills of diagnosis, prescription, treatment, and evaluation to help develop existing human resources? Specifically, the facilitative leader uses each element as a step in the process of planned change. There are two objectives of the diagnosis process: identification of the problem or problems, and identification of resources which can contribute to the solutions. In moving educational systems toward improvement, the leader facilitates people to identify the problems which are of most importance to them. What are the needs of young people in our community? What are the educational desires and needs of the community population? To what extent does our present educational system meet these needs? To what extent does it not? Answers to these questions form the foundation of the diagnostic phase of the process. Through consistent dialogue with students, teachers and community members, the facilitative leader can help identify specific problems which must be solved to implement productive educational change.

Once the problem has been defined, all people involved should begin to identify those resources which can be brought to bear on the solution. Assessment of resources falls into three categories: those of the education system, i.e., teachers, administrators, district staff, board members; those of the community, i.e., citizens, social agencies, government and other institutions; and those of the community educator, i.e., leadership skills and techniques. In an age where communities are so diverse and pluralistic, one is only limited by his or her own imagination in identifying potential resources and bringing them into harmony with the existing system through leadership to more efficiently meet identified needs. By clarifying communication between the system and its clients, the community educator facilitates more concise goals, thus problem-solving and decision-making will become a united effort between those who serve and those to be served.

The result of the diagnostic process brings the participants to a point wherein they collectively prescribe methods to facilitate appropriate institutional change necessary to meet the defined needs. In prescribing methods for change, the leader(s) should become familiar with the typologies of Robert Chin, a noted psychologist and change theorist. They are stated by Chin as being: empirical-rational strategies, normative reeducative strategies, and power strategies.[4] The methods included in these typologies can be categorized basically as *persuasion, intervention* and *power-related.* In prescribing methods for inducing change, using Chin's typologies, it is necessary to identify the specific objectives to be achieved for the clients and the system.

The empirical-rational approach is based on persuasive techniques. Its basic premise is that people are reasonable and will act in a rational and logical manner in accepting change *if* one can demonstrate obvious need for change and indicate the benefits to be derived. Using this strategy, the community educator would rely on such activities as conferences, visitations, media presentations, personal advocacy by those who have already experienced community education, and expert consultations to move individuals toward an operational philosophy of community education. Through these and other such activities, the community educator can facilitate development of some common knowledge on which the individuals within the institutions can base their rational judgments concerning community education.

The normative-reeducative strategies are based on direct intervention within the system. Efforts must be made to activate forces within the system to evolve the desired changes through collaborative work. Such activities as developing a citizens' council or special task force for educational improvement could be employed. In addition, one could conduct special workshop encounters to develop problem-solving techniques or to provide activities in group leadership, group guidance and human relations training. All of these types of transactional activities are basically designed to help the individual involved establish a positive attitude toward cooperation and collaboration. Whatever treatment is chosen, it must be provided for all those involved in the change process. These direct interventions should be oriented toward modifying attitudes and beliefs in an attempt to involve the participants to a point of emotional commitment to total community education.

Finally, the third approach is the one most often used, but least often acknowledged — power strategies. Quite often, power implies negative forces and is associated with leader-centered behavior. It is usually thought to be essentially a concept of compliance and submission to change. However, this evaluation only holds true if the force of compliance is from the top of the organizational power structure down. Governing bodies, school boards, city councils, etc., cannot successfully force their subordinates into productive community education endeavors. Mandated change is seldom productive or lasting. The commitment must come from the bottom up. A grassroots approach is consistently more lasting because it has the support of those who must implement the change: teachers, students, and community members. With this in mind, the leader can work with these latent power sources to facilitate their efforts to influence the formal organizational structure of the serving institutions. To meet the collective needs and desires of those to be served, these latent power sources must bring about a redistribution of institutional resources. The facilitative leader can promote attempts by these groups to influence institutional leadership into a cooperative attitude conducive to community education. Since institutions were created to serve the community, those to be served should use every legitimate power they can develop to bring about the desired change.

In brief, one can see that the various methodologies described could be most effectively utilized if an eclectic approach were to be taken. However, one must relate each subsystem with the activities best suited to the conditions as they are perceived. Above all, the interpersonal skills of facilitative leadership, effective listening, genuineness, understanding, respect, intelligence, and interpersonal communication, can assist the community educator in developing strategies for affecting the attitudes of the individuals with whom he deals, and, hopefully, can assist in building a common commitment to community education at all levels.

Once treatment activities are employed, it is essential that their progress be monitored by evaluation techniques. Evaluation should be conducted in terms of the specific objectives identified during the prescriptive phase. In addition, to determine how well the activity meets the identified objectives, it is often useful to evaluate the treatment methodology to ascertain if the process were carried out as desired. The results of such formative evaluation may be used for planning of additional activities or for improving diagnosis through redefinition of the issues to be addressed.

Through the use of these identified skills and techniques the leader can facilitate increasing awareness of and interest in community education. Once the awareness has been established, emergent leadership from the group can be effectively channeled to produce the shared leadership so essential to adoption of change.

The two basic leadership approaches discussed in the preceding paragraphs are very different from each other. The leader-centered style is by far the most expedient and simplest to manage because leadership is vested primarily in one person, the status leader. This commonly utilized approach is the faster of the two in goal identification, plan of action selection, and in delivery of programs. The other-centered, or facilitative style, is less expedient and more difficult to manage because it vests leadership in many people. Probably the leader-centered is the more common of the two styles because it is easier. To be simple and expedient, however, does not imply that it is the more effective approach. Conversely, its over-utilization has contributed to some of our major problems in education. The leader-centered style appears to have taken us away from basic principles of involvement. Public educational institutions, like our nation itself, are "of the people, by the people, for the people." If significant educational change is to take place, it is essential for "the people" to be physically and emotionally involved. We seem to have evolved into a situation wherein the tail is wagging the dog. Employes of educational systems, rather than the people they serve, have established the direction and scope of educational endeavors. As educational leaders, we should not direct others toward the preconceived goals we have established, but rather assist them in determining their own goals and the scope of their endeavors.

Shared leadership is the key element for positive change in both the quality and quantity of services provided by our educational institutions. Facilitative leadership and resultant shared leadership provide for continuity, acceptance, and maximum utilization of human potential. Facilitative leadership is the more sophisticated approach. It requires far more empathy, genuineness, listening, respect for clients, knowledge of leadership, and skills in interpersonal communications. These skills are not rapidly acquired, but must be learned over an extended period of time. Specific training is badly needed and should be provided to potential leaders. The basic components of this leadership style should be an integral part of all administrative and leadership training programs.

Facilitative leadership is a low profile style of leadership that assists "the people" to determine what they desire and need from their respective educational institutions and then helps them assume a contributing role in meeting these identified desires and needs. Community education is education "of the people, by the people, for the people." Facilitative leadership is clearly the style most appropriate in community education because it vests leadership and responsibility in these same people.

Yet leadership, however creative, constructive and effective, is not enough to assure significant curriculum reconstruction. To leadership must be added many and varied institutional and community resources upon which leaders may draw. That is why resources for curriculum change are the concern of the following chapter.

7. RESOURCES FOR CURRICULUM CHANGE

The most distinguishing mark of the new educational program is its close involvement with the life of the entire community. The richness of its program will reach all the people at convenient times and places with offerings adapted to their interests and needs. The education centered community provides education for all. It not only helps people but it also helps people to help themselves. In the school of such a community and in its varied community life, much of the teaching and leadership comes from the people themselves. In the process of helping others they educate themselves . . .

Education can *meet the expectations of the American people. It* can *help our nation to cope with its crisis, but to do so it must recognize the obsolescence of many of our assumptions and practices . . .*

The current crisis of education is ample evidence that we have waited too long to bring about the change that is needed. It is possible that failure to move or a move that is made too slowly may change the path of American Freedom. Our nation has been strong because the people have been able to make rapid change and to meet all emergencies. Disaster can be avoided by enlisting the leadership of those who determine educational destiny in discarding outmoded beliefs and practices and adopting the new role for education.

— V. M. Kerensky and Ernest O. Melby,
Education II: The Social Imperative

There are many ways through which to bring about positive change in a system of education. These ways range from slight modification of present programs to creating anarchy and then rebuilding from the resulting rubble. Curricular change will undoubtedly be most effective when it is gradual yet continuous and retains the best of our current endeavors. The challenge before us is similar to that of the prison superintendent who was directed to build a new prison out of the building blocks of the old prison, yet not hamper its ongoing operations. The challenge of reconstructing a new curriculum from the materials of the old is undoubtedly equally as difficult. It is, however, the only realistic approach.

The ideas and suggestions which follow should not be perceived as solutions, but rather as grist for the mill of discussion, evaluation, and implementation.

EXISTING RESOURCES

Assuming that our goal is to develop a system of education based on community education and a curriculum centered on lifelong needs, what then are some of the more common resources currently available for initiating positive change? They include boards of education, administrators, teachers, community members, individual school centers, schools and colleges of education, state departments of education, and centers for community education development.

Boards of Education

Boards of education and individual board members are very important resources for curriculum reform because they are in a position to set policy which affects direction and emphasis of public school education. They wield tremendous potential since they are capable, in a single act, of establishing policies that can become the foundation for development of life-centered curricula.

Board members should be provided opportunity to explore community education and curriculum centered on life concerns. Too often, board members are criticized for their lack of understanding and support of new ideas, yet are not given experiences to broaden their thinking. It is important to provide inservice training on a regular basis through visitations, brainstorming retreats, and other informal means. Hopefully, from such experiences, board members will assume leadership in policy formulation that facilitates curriculum reform.

Obviously, policies affecting curriculum can be written many ways and have different emphases. Such components as the following should be considered for inclusion in statements of school policy:

Official commitment to provide various kinds of learning opportunities for community members of all ages and interests;

Official commitment to the systematic utilization of representative community members in identifying desires and needs which might be met through school and other educational programs and services;

Official commitment to the maximum utilization of community members and other community resources in all learning endeavors;

Official commitment to provide learning experiences to school-age youth that are centered around real life concerns, such as those previously identified and discussed;

Official commitment to cooperate and coordinate efforts with other institutions, agencies and organizations.

In order for policy statements to be of value in curriculum reform, they must be carefully thought out and well written. They should be absolute statements of the direction and emphasis desired by the board of education. Statements of policy can be of value only when they are well prepared and clearly perceived as board expectations by the professional education staff which is vested with the responsibility of implementation.

Board of education members can be a valuable resource in curriculum reform. The key factor in nurturing this potential lies in inservice training. Board members need planned opportunities to explore future needs of the community, to examine existing program endeavors, and to broaden their own conceptual skills. Inservice training is as important for board members as it is for professional staff.

Administrators

The authors' inquiry to Centers for Community Education across the nation identified many line and staff administrators who are providing leadership in curriculum reform. There are undoubtedly countless others who believe the school curriculum should focus on the lifelong concerns of its participants and could provide such leadership.

Included in this major category of school personnel are all administrators, advisors, directors and coordinators. They may be grouped into two categories: those who are in line administrative positions; and those with staff administrative responsibility.

Line administrators are all administrative staff members who have supervisory roles in relationship to other school employes. Included in this group are superintendents, assistant superintendents, selected other central administrators, and principals.

These administrators can facilitate the acceptance of community education and curriculum reform in many ways. Initially, the central office administrators can provide learning opportunities for board of education members in order to help them become more familiar with community education and life-centered curricula. This might be achieved through such activities as visitation to ongoing programs, exploration with resource people, participation in brainstorming sessions, and increased involvement with community council members. Secondly, line administrators can also help in the formulation of proposed statements of policy for board action. Such proposals, when adopted, would become the policy for curriculum direction and emphasis. Line administrators who work at individual centers are also good resources for curriculum reform. Principals and other school center administrators, working with their respective staff members and community council representatives, can facilitate comprehensive planning for their respective centers. These plans should reflect the basic principles of community education and direct greater emphasis to the utilization of community members and community resources in program endeavors.

Both central and school center administrators can help develop incentives and establish machinery to encourage staff members to examine future needs, participate in experimental curriculum endeavors, and utilize a community and life-centered emphasis in the learning experiences they provide. They can also work closely with community councils in direction-setting, securing ideas for increased involvement of community members and resources, and in facilitating communication.

There are many other ways for line administrators to facilitate curriculum reform. Because of the supervisory status they have in their respective institutions, they have the opportunity to take initiative in working with staff members in curriculum evaluation and modification.

Those individuals in the second category, staff administrators, include all coordinators and directors who have administrative responsibilities but are not in supervisory roles. Curriculum personnel are here grouped with staff administrators because, in most cases, they too are administrators without supervisory responsibility. Also included in this category are people who provide consultant and training services to faculty members. Roles of these staff administrators may range from assistant superintendents to teacher-cluster leaders.

Staff administrators can be valuable resource people in curriculum reform because of the unique role they play in their respective institutions. Most curriculum personnel, as well as many other staff administrators, are responsible for assisting faculty members by providing them consultant and training services. Because of this, they have opportunity to affect curriculum in many ways.

One way for curriculum planners and staff administrators to influence curriculum reconstruction is to provide systematic inservice training for staff members and, in many cases, extend such training opportunities to selected community members. It is probably obvious that learning experiences designed to broaden conceptual insights, reduce adherence to tradition, and create an atmosphere of evaluation and modification should be extended to the maximum possible number of people. These administrators can provide much leadership through well-planned inservice training. Community education and curriculum based on life concerns should be emphasized in such training. Through inservice training, teachers can receive training in the effective utilization of community members and other community resources in the institution's educational endeavors, both in and out of classrooms.

A second major area for contribution by these staff administrators exists in their consultant roles. These leaders can, in their helper capacities, work with individual teachers and teaching teams on curriculum matters and, more specifically as these teachers address themselves to goals, upon plans of action, nature of experience provided, and evaluation. During this process, many seeds of change can be planted and nurtured. The role played by the administrator should not be leader-centered, but rather one that helps facilitate members of the group to address themselves to the immediate and future needs of their clients. Such facilitative leadership invests greatly in the creative thinking of each teacher and in the group as a whole. Overall, this can help teachers and others understand that curriculum evaluation and change must be a continuous process because the needs of students are ever-changing. The importance of teacher leadership and participation in assessing needs and in developing means for meeting them can also be emphasized. This point will be explored in depth later in this chapter.

The nature of teacher involvement is very important. Teachers should not be lectured to or coerced, but rather they should have important and active roles to play in curriculum endeavors. Furthermore, every attempt should be made to help them receive inservice training concurrent with their group involvement.

A third way for staff administrators to facilitate curriculum reform is through resource utilization. They can encourage greater community member involvement and resource utilization in instructional endeavors by assisting in identifying and securing people who are willing to serve as resources. These administrators can assist teachers, directly or indirectly, by acquiring information on human and physical resources available in the community and by developing a cataloging and retrieval system. They might also provide coordinating services through one or another school office. Such services might direct teachers to contact a central source, which in turn would attempt to secure use of the desired resources. This clearing house function should be designed to minimize teacher effort, to avoid overuse and overcontact, to provide follow up, and to maintain current information listings.

A fourth suggested way for staff administrators to facilitate reform focuses on curriculum materials themselves. The old axiom, "We teach as we have been taught," can be extended to read, "and merely use revisions of the same old materials." Unfortunately, curriculum materials have changed little over the past several decades. New hardware has affected the means of delivering information. However, the information continues to focus on academic subject matter. It is also unfortunate that a large number of teachers rely very heavily on prepared materials and develop little on their own. There exists a real need for development of visual, audio and written materials that focus on lifelong needs of students in this revolutionary period of history. Many of these materials can be prepared by local faculty members. Staff administrators can encourage and assist in their development.

Individual Teachers and Teaching Teams

Teachers are one of the most important resources for facilitating curriculum reform. Any attempt to bring about curriculum change without utilizing the cooperation of teachers will be ineffective. Throughout our nation there are countless teachers and teaching teams who are distressed and dissatisfied with current curriculum endeavors and who believe that curriculum should be based directly on life concerns of their students. Many of these teachers realize that they are in positions to affect curriculum and have initiated, or are initiating, steps towards such changes. In preparation of this book, Centers for Community Education throughout the nation were asked to identify areas and personnel demonstrating the application of basic principles of community education of existing elementary and secondary curricula. In response, many individual teachers were cited and narratives of their endeavors included. A broad spectrum of activities was listed. However, most centered around teacher-initiated involvement of community members and introduction of community resources into the classroom learning experiences, as well as the systematic involvement of youth out of the classroom and into their respective communities. It is obvious that teachers are in a position to serve both as catalysts for change and as change agents. Their endeavors can be unilateral, or developed in cooperation with curriculum committees. Hopefully, good curriculum leadership will exist so that teacher efforts need not be unilateral.

Teachers are an important resource for facilitating curriculum reform because they are the front-line troops. In most cases, they are able to choose the nature of learning experiences utilized to meet established goals. They can build toward a life-centered curriculum by involving community members and community resources in the everyday learning experiences of youth. Direct involvement of community members with their diverse interests, backgrounds and occupations will help to break down the conventional book-learning approach and provide learning opportunities that reflect more closely the life concerns and needs of community members, and so make the educative process more personally meaningful to the participants.

Increased parent involvement in school learning activities can be initiated by teachers in order to help parents become more aware of classroom goals; to encourage parents to work with the teachers in achieving these goals, and to provide opportunity for parents to work closely with trained staff in establishing future goals which are based on mutually identified needs. A major by-product of parent involvement is the opportunity for informal parent education.

Another opportune area for teacher influence on curriculum centers around the selected emphasis in presenting various conventional subject areas. Within the subject areas themselves, most teachers have much freedom to influence the nature of learning experiences and organization of study. For example, within the subject field of social studies, teachers could develop units that would relate directly to lifelong concerns. One such unit might focus on man's inability to get along with his fellow man. Bigotry, racism, warfare, and other forms of aggression and prejudice could be studied. Another unit might be directed toward societal problem-solving. Teachers could involve youth directly in identifying community problems, working with existing resources, and formulating procedures for refining major problems into smaller component parts. Finally, students could be assisted in the identification, examination and application of alternative plans of action toward solving common community problems.

Freedom to influence the nature of learning experiences and organization of study exists in any subject area. For example, the study of biological sciences could emphasize the practical application of those aspects that relate most directly to good health and to people living successfully in their environment. Human ecology, environmental degradation and destruction, balance of nature, and the prevention and treatment of illness — all would be important aspects to include in such a core unit. Physical education, on the other hand, might emphasize lifelong physical well-being through individual exercises and sports. Awareness and skill building in lifelong individualized sports — such as tennis, golf, bowling and jogging — could serve as a core and allow team activities to become a complement rather than the overwhelming focus of attention.

The curriculum can be affected greatly by teachers within the parameters of their roles. An experienced teacher once responded to a new teacher who was complaining that he lacked opportunity to change curriculum by stating, "First, close your classroom door, and then your mouth, and you will have the opportunity." While this approach is not necessarily advocated, some truth does exist in the implications of that statement. Many worthwhile curriculum endeavors have had premature observation and articulation, to their later demise. Care should be taken in planning well each endeavor and then, when implemented, in letting it be worked, evaluated, and modified without premature publicity. Curriculum change should emphasize systematic modification and evaluation toward defensible goals, rather than mere experimentation. Very few people desire to have their children or themselves serve as guinea pigs for trial programs. Experiments are essential, but experimenters should beware of the trial and error environment which often accompanies experimental curriculum endeavors.

Individual teachers and teaching teams are probably the most important resource for facilitating curriculum reform. Participants in a workshop examining school curriculum needs of the 1980s concluded that "Teachers share with members of all professions a tendency to be conservative in outlook and a reluctance to adopt radical change."[1] Yet, every member of the workshop was convinced that "Any attempt to bring about change without the willing cooperation of teachers would be utterly ineffective." They went on to say that "To secure this cooperation and to win their (teacher) support for reforms that are necessary to meet the needs of education in the 1980's, it will be essential to insure that there is a two-way relationship between teachers and curriculum developers." They also concluded that "No less significant for success is the provision of inservice education for teachers on a systematic and regular basis."

A high-quality teacher inservice training program on a regular basis is essential in curriculum reform. In order to implement a life-centered curriculum, new conceptual and technical skills need to be acquired by the classroom teacher.

Community Members

Other important, yet quite often overlooked, resources for curriculum reform are community people with their diverse interests, past experiences, talents and willingness to share. Community members are so important because they can contribute in many different ways. Three ways may serve as examples.

The first of these is through their involvement on community councils. Such councils should be a functional part of each and every school. These councils should address themselves to the total learning desires and needs of the communities they serve. Community councils are the very heart of the community educational process. Community members can contribute to curriculum changes through their systematic involvement in identifying needs, establishing resultant educational goals, assisting educators in the achievement of these goals, and in evaluation. School leaders should encourage them to identify and discuss the life concerns of the people they represent and make recommendations to school officials. Community members can contribute much to curriculum evaluation and modification when involved on *real* community councils. Such councils should be delegated the major piece of the action and be allowed to function at their full potential.

Another possible way for community members to affect curriculum is through their direct involvement in educational endeavors as resource people. Community members, with their diverse life experiences, talents, and interests, can be utilized throughout the program. For example, teachers leading a study on other countries or continents can involve community members who have traveled through some of these lands and possibly taken pictures or movies which can be shared. There are probably other community members who may have come from these areas and can share their language, collected artifacts, and knowledge of dress, food, customs and values. Utilization of these community members would enrich any learning experience, and, at the same time, potentially encourage feelings of worth for the individuals involved.

Another example of community-member involvement as resource people relates to life experiences. Many community members can be resources because of their past experience. Teachers of history can involve community members who have participated in historical events, such as the Great Depression, the attack on Pearl Harbor, the Asian war resistance movement, a recent political campaign, and the like. Older lifelong residents of the community can share pictures and memories of what the community was like during different periods of time or where businesses which no longer exist were once located and the roles played by them in the community's history. Obviously, community members also can share their knowledge of skills that relate to their occupations or special interests.

Many people have criticized schools for their poor utilization of the physical and financial resources available to them. Yet, even more gross is their waste of the human talent available in their respective communities. Community members can enrich so many learning experiences and simultaneously enrich the nature and scope of the curriculum.

A final suggestion relates directly to parent-teacher organizations. Many parent-teacher organization meetings appear to evolve away from their original intent — to facilitate communication between parents and teachers and improve instruction for children.

Parent-teacher groups often seem to be so preoccupied with school carnivals and other money-raising events that little or no time or energy remains for discussing learning endeavors. Many such events are worthwhile projects, but often they divert attention from vital instructional problems. Leadership needs to be provided to refocus the emphasis, to stress improvement of communication and of learning endeavors. Parent-teacher groups should also begin to discuss the life concerns of people and how some of these might be better met through the school curriculum.

Individual School Centers

Thus far the potential of individuals in effecting curriculum reform has been discussed. People *are* the key to curriculum change because school buildings and institutions do not think or lead. Only people possess this ability. Therefore, as we examine the potential for elementary, middle, and secondary schools to improve curriculum, let us keep in mind that we are talking about centers for learning which include students, faculty, parents, and other community people.

Individual school centers (schools) are excellent resources for curriculum reform because they are the functional units of the school system. As such they have the flexibility necessary for inservice training, comprehensive planning, and experimentation. The importance of inservice education for faculty members has already been emphasized. Much of this training can be effectively accomplished with an entire staff of the school center. From such training, faculty members can increase their conceptual and technical skills which are so essential for curriculum reform. Inservice training activities should be continuous and stress utilization of community resources in curriculum endeavors.

Comprehensive planning is another important activity which can contribute significantly to curriculum evaluation and modification. Such planning should involve both faculty and community members in the development of educational objectives that focus on providing community-centered learning experiences for people of all ages. These objectives should emanate from a multisource assessment of community member desires and needs. Also discussed in comprehensive planning should be alternative ways to achieve stated objectives and evaluation procedures. A comprehensive plan, when properly utilized, becomes the plan of action from which the faculty of a school center can operate. All services and programs provided by a school center would be included in the plan. The day school then becomes but one part of the total program. Every attempt should be made to involve faculty of the school center in its total educational endeavor and to discourage fragmentation or isolation.

Overall, comprehensive planning is a good way to examine current and future needs, alter or develop new objectives, and apply creativity to program and service endeavors.

Once a comprehensive plan is developed, it becomes the responsibility of the principal and selected educators to determine staffing roles and possible reassignment of existing faculty. Volunteers should be utilized to assist the professional staff members.

Another effective and relatively simple way to facilitate curriculum change is to periodically offer noncredit enrichment classes during the school day. These special days are an opportunity for school-age youth to participate in short courses of their interest in general topic areas such as crafts, culinary arts, dance, electronics, music, mechanics, astronomy, literature, photography, and recreation. These and other topics of special interest are usually identified by students, parents, and other community members. Such minicourses are usually offered for an entire day every four to eight weeks. Participation in these funtastic Fridays, as they are sometimes called, provides a good opportunity for everybody involved to see the range of activities which can take place at a school, to see that faculty members often have other special interests and skills in addition to their subject fields, and to see that many community members can serve as resource people and contribute to the learning of others.

These special enrichment days can play a most significant role in changing people's attitudes toward schooling and toward learning in general. However, such programs must be carefully planned and executed. Care must be taken because small organizational and administrative problems could become big problems and destroy or impede this valuable endeavor.

Experimentation is obviously a very important aspect of curriculum reform. It provides the opportunity to identify both strengths and weaknesses of prospective curriculum innovations. School centers can and should encourage systematic experimentation by faculty members with assistance from curriculum personnel. Many good ideas get panned before their relative merits are ever known. Careful experimentation is an excellent way to control such premature reactions and give each idea or innovation opportunity to be proved and improved. Schools have a responsibility to their consumers to evaluate the relative strengths and weaknesses of all school endeavors.

Research and development (R&D) has been identified by the business and professional communities as being essential; yet, it hardly exists at school centers even though school centers appear to be the sites most appropriate for controlled experimentation. Schools have immense responsibility to carry on continuous research and development in order to best meet the immediate and future needs of their clients. To paraphrase Marshall McLuhan: "We must direct our attention less to the rearview mirror of the past and instead look through the front windshield to the future, even though it represents the unknown." Innovative programs and individual ideas should be tested to determine their relative merits. Modifications should be made where there are weaknesses. Obviously, some of these ideas and innovations will prove to be ineffective, inappropriate, or far too costly. Others which seemed far out will demonstrate their value. Such experimentation can contribute significantly to curriculum reform because every program or idea has the opportunity to stand on its own merit.

Many experimental endeavors at school centers were identified in the brief national survey conducted by the authors. Most of these related to experimentation in classroom approach, although several others dealt with subject matter grouping. Only a small number were measuring the effects of significant utilization of community resources in instructional endeavors. None was experimenting directly with curriculum based on enduring life concerns.

Current experimentation has led to the establishment of various kinds of "alternative schools" throughout the nation. These programs vary greatly in nature and scope. Some are directed to the needs of youth in trouble or who have been removed from the regular school program. These are sometimes seen by their protagonists as dumping-ground operations. Others see them as alternatives to traditional programs which have already failed to meet the needs of these youngsters. Many other alternative schools are making curriculum changes of mode or operation. Some of these endeavors receive assistance from the National Alternative Schools Program, a University of Massachusetts' project supported by the United States Office of Education. Among its aims, NASP is committed to: ". . . promoting options within the public school system that allow for voluntary participation by students, staff, parents, and community; creating schools that recognize the validity of special environments for students and communities with unique learning needs or goals, and developing multi-racial education programs that encourage respect for cultural and socio-economic diversity."[2]

Hopefully, all alternative plans result from high-quality systematic experimentation. It would appear, however, that often they are in the trial-and-error business, using real kids as their subjects.

A final suggested way for school centers to facilitate curriculum change relates to career education. Many people feel that schools have a responsibility to do far more than they have been doing in career awareness and preparation. Yet schools are not equipped, nor do they have the human resources within their staff, to provide the experience needed. A sound, comprehensive career education program requires mutual planning by business officials, labor unions, governmental representatives, school people, and other community members. It also requires cooperation among educational institutions, involvement at business sites, and cost sharing. Such mutual planning and programming would have a significant effect on curriculum.

School centers can and should use career education and endeavors of similar need and magnitude to meet desired goals and indirectly change curriculum. There is, however, a caution to be observed. Both school faculty members and community people should be involved throughout the process, for, in order to have a successful career curriculum, they must become emotionally committed.

School centers have potential to facilitate curriculum reconstruction. But school centers as such cannot accomplish this. *People* are the key to change, not facilities or institutions.

Schools and Colleges of Education

Schools and colleges of education are the teacher preparation institutions. They have for the most part focused most of their efforts on *preparation* programs for teachers, counselors and administrators and have focused very little on serving them later while they are on the job. The term "teacher preparation institutions" depicts well the role played by most. The emphasis has been placed on the readying of people for a job with little concern for assisting them throughout their professional careers. Obviously this approach directly reflects the formulas established to finance colleges of education. Most receive funds according to their ability to generate student credit hours. As important as funding is, it is not the sole culprit! Colleges of education have traditionally perceived themselves as preparation institutions having little or no responsibility for assisting educators (except for those involved in formal graduate training) on the job. The educator shortage, which existed for many years, perpetuated this role. Now, however, there is no shortage, and so there is less need for quantity.

Colleges of education should reevaluate their endeavors and place greater emphasis on helping educators throughout their careers. *Career education should be careerlong*! Many other professions recognize this and have developed systems for continued inservice training. Colleges of education should also recognize the need for careerlong training and work closely with educators and their employing institutions to plan jointly for continued educational experiences. Funding is not the barrier to career life training. Funding formulas can be altered. The real barriers are in the feelings and minds of people.

Colleges of education can and should play a significant role in curriculum reconstruction. If anything, it is one of their major responsibilities. Colleges that subscribe to a careerlong approach can provide assistance both on campus and out in the field. One valid assumption is that teachers can best be trained when teacher preparation institutions work in consort with school districts to provide a campus-field approach over an extended period of time.

Concerning undergraduate teacher preparation, teachers in training should be required early in their programs to examine firsthand the philosophical concept of community education and its basic components. Learning experiences should be developed that demonstrate the importance of systematic involvement of community members in the total educational process; maximum utilization of all human, physical and financial resources of a community; interinstitutional and agency cooperation and coordination; lifelong learning experiences for community members of all ages; democratic involvement of community members in problem-solving; and educational programs and services that are based upon and centered in the enduring life concerns of people.

Another suggestion is that colleges of education not leave curriculum teaching to subject area specialists. Professional educators should take a direct role in exposing potential teachers to curriculum development, evaluation, and revision. It is probably more important for teachers to have an overall understanding of curriculum development than it is for them to apply curriculum principles to a particular subject field. It is especially appropriate to help these teachers in training, regardless of their specialization, to examine curricula based upon the enduring life concerns of people.

Greater emphasis should also be placed on technical instruction for teaching various age groups of community members. Vast numbers of teachers will be needed to instruct community members from preschool age to older adults. Teachers in training should have specific instruction in the teaching of preschool children, early and later elementary youth, secondary students, and adults at different age levels, including senior citizens.Teaching methods appropriate for elementary or secondary students can be quite inappropriate for others.

Utilization of community members and community resources in instructional endeavors is another essential training element which ought to be incorporated in teacher preparation programs. Teachers in training should not only be interning in the schools but also in the communities served by the schools. The teachers should become well acquainted, in some depth, with their respective communities. This acquaintance might be accomplished by having them intern with one or more municipal agencies and/or with community school leaders.

Colleges of education are obviously in positions to significantly affect curriculum research and development. These have for a long time been considered desirable functions of teacher preparation institutions. Unfortunately, many research findings which could improve school curriculum are not implemented or even tried. A major gap seems to exist between research and development and implementation. More effort must be placed on dissemination and training.

There are also many ways for colleges of education to contribute through their graduate endeavors to curriculum improvement. Without attempting to describe an ideal graduate program, the following suggestions are offered to enhance current endeavors.

One of the most important needs of schools, colleges, universities, and other educational institutions and agencies is that of educational leadership. Quality leadership is badly needed in all facets of education. Unfortunately, many people equate educational leadership with school administration. School administrators do need to be effective leaders, but they should not be expected to provide all the leadership essential for excellence in educational programming. Leadership must be vested in many people, rather than in status leaders only. Colleges of education are in excellent positions to provide high-quality leadership training to participants of various programs. Such training endeavors should emphasize facilitative leadership which, in brief, focuses on the participants rather than on the leaders. This leadership approach stimulates members of the group to emerge and to assume responsibility. Graduate programs should provide opportunity for their participants to learn the conceptual and technical skills necessary to lead others in needs assessment, goals setting, program development and evaluation.

A second suggestion relates to the preparation of administrators. An earlier section of this chapter discussed many ways for line and staff administrators to contribute to curriculum reconstruction. Administrators cannot be expected to achieve these without adequate training. Potential administrators should be expected to demonstrate the skills necessary to facilitate curriculum change. Emphasis should be placed not only on contemporary conceptual and technical skill development, but also on community education, the role of education in different social settings, and on life concerns of community members. Again, much effort should be placed on individual leadership skill building.

Many of these comments are also applicable to the training of curriculum personnel and teachers. Colleges of education can have an indirect effect on school curriculum and classroom approach through their preparation of these important leaders. Emphasis should be placed on procedures and techniques for curriculum development, based upon enduring life concerns and utilization of community resources in instructional endeavors.

Leadership training in community education can also contribute to later curriculum reform. Currently, community education personnel serve as facilitators for change. They are usually providing leadership to bring together more closely the school, community members, and the institutions and agencies that provide educational services. Special training is needed to ready people to assume these important change agent roles. Training in community education should not, however, be restricted to these persons. School administrators, curriculum personnel, counselors, and teachers — all should have opportunity to examine the concept and its application. Every participant in a graduate education program should be exposed to this operational philosophy of education and its basic components. People really involved in community education often become very much aware of what they personally can do to effect improvement in education.

As already noted, schools and colleges of education place most of their efforts on preparation programs for teachers, counselors and administrators. Very little concern is shown to assist these educators throughout their professional careers. Colleges of education need to recognize the inadequacies of such a limited program and to initiate plans for comprehensive career follow-up. The time seems appropriate for such a change in direction because enrollments in many teacher preparation institutions are leveling off or declining. Projections indicate this trend will continue for a considerable period of time. With this de-emphasis on quantity, college faculty members should have increasingly more time to develop high-quality programs and services.

Colleges of education are beginning to identify the importance of outreach. There appears to be increasing awareness that professional educators need continued training and assistance in order to keep up with changing times. Education colleges should increasingly commit faculty, programs, and services to systematic outreach. Ideally, colleges of education should provide both quality preparation programs and career follow-up services through a combination of campus and field experiences. This can best be achieved through philosophic change and retraining of staff, good leadership, promotional and/or salary incentives. All are essential.

Two of the most valuable outreach services which can be provided by colleges of education are consultation and training, since both are natural extensions of these institutions. Consultant assistance should be provided schools, colleges, universities and other community education agencies without charge or at minimal costs. Consultation should be considered a regular function of college faculty. College professors should be expected to share their expertise with institutions within the service area as a regular function of their professional role. Their role should be one of helper rather than that of direct leadership or of a "tell them how to do it" attitude.

Inservice training in curriculum design is also a natural extension of colleges of education and can be valuable to both the recipients and the colleges themselves. Quality training is badly needed in the field. Colleges can benefit from faculty awareness of field needs and use the training as a possible feeder system to graduate programs. Inservice training can be formal or informal, with or without credit, structured into classes or handled on an individual basis. Such inservice training need not be expensive, since many of the human resources needed probably are already employed by the participating institutions. Funds can also be acquired from credit hour generation, inservice training budgets, and federal, state and local project monies. Training should not be something packaged by colleges of education to take on the road. It should be jointly planned by faculty of all institutions involved.

Educator preparation institutions can also develop special outreach functions designed to provide consultation and training services in specific areas. For example, approximately seventy Centers for Community Education have been developed by colleges and universities across the nation. These centers, funded by their respective institutions and grant monies, provide direct assistance to schools, colleges, universities and other agencies through consultation and training. They have had and will continue to have a tremendous impact on the growth and development of community education. Their potential will be discussed in greater depth later in this chapter.

Other kinds of centers and functions can be established to meet specific needs of education institutions. Some of the special outreach functions already in existence provide assistance in areas such as career education, school finance, curriculum, humanistic studies, gerontology, school facility planning, research and development. Teacher corps projects are also beginning to focus on continued inservice needs of educators already in the field.

Two very important outreach services which colleges of education can provide are research and development. The need for quality experimentation has already been mentioned. Colleges should develop well-budgeted research and development centers with staff members who desire to work closely with people in the field. Educational research and development are mutual responsibilities of colleges of education and elementary-secondary schools. These institutions in consort have the human, physical and financial resources necessary to maintain quality research and development.

State Departments of Education

State departments of education can be valuable resources in curriculum reform. Their potential, however, depends greatly on how well they are received by the institutions they serve. Most departments are respected and in positions of influence. In many areas they are providing leadership in curriculum evaluation and improvement.

State departments of education can contribute in many ways to the increased acceptance of community education and life-centered curriculum. First of all, the departments themselves can serve as models for community education in action by encouraging and exhibiting cooperation among their respective divisions. They can also demonstrate maximum utilization of all human, physical and financial resources available to them by working closely with other state agencies, such as health and rehabilitative services, conservation offices, penal and judicial services, commerce departments, and social services.

A second way state departments of education can be of assistance is by providing high-quality consultation and training services in curriculum evaluation and modification. Training workshops can be provided for teachers, administrators, and community members that are designed to increase both their conceptual insights and technical skills.

Another way for them to assist in curriculum reform is by encouraging experimentation and development of on-site models. Both are essential in curriculum revision. Incentives could be created to encourage school centers and districts to examine their current curriculum activities and develop new programs or approaches. Grant monies, made available through proposal submission, might serve as such an incentive. School centers and districts contributing to curriculum enrichment through experimentation could receive other special recognition, such as awards, tributes, and adulations. Obviously, other incentives could be established to encourage and facilitate improvement of curriculum. Departments of education could assist local district experimental endeavors by providing consultation and training services. They could also develop and distribute visual, audio and written materials which assist in curriculum revision.

Centers for Community Education Development

Centers for Community Education development are an important resource for facilitating curriculum change. Approximately seventy such Centers (see Appendix A, Number 6) have thus far been established throughout the nation by colleges, universities and state departments of education to provide consultation and training services at no costs to the recipients. These Centers have been very successful in facilitating acceptance and implementation of community education through their eight primary services:

To provide information on community education;

To provide consultant assistance in developing and implementing community education;

To provide ideas for securing financial assistance;

To provide aid in securing and training community education personnel;

To provide preservice and inservice training opportunities;

To provide assistance in evaluation of community education;

To provide undergraduate and graduate training in community education; and

To provide information on additional consultation and training services available.

Additional Centers are needed, since the current ones can only begin to serve the nation adequately. More important than the number of Centers is the quality of staff. All Centers need to be staffed with well-trained, futuristic, change-facilitating leaders. Staff members with limited knowledge of community education and its basic components can do far more harm than good. Greater emphasis needs to be placed on the *training of trainers*. The potential of Centers for Community Education to facilitate curriculum change is great. Important as they are, however, such Centers should be established only as rapidly as competent staff members are trained for their unique leadership responsibilities.

BRAINSTORMED SUGGESTIONS

Thus far in this chapter, several existing resources have been identified and some of the ways each can contribute to curriculum improvement have been indicated. In an attempt to provide readers with many more ideas for consideration and discussion, the authors involved nine people (see Appendix B) in two extended brainstorming sessions. These participants were asked to identify various measures that could be taken to affect school curriculum. No attempt was made to discuss the relative merits of each of their suggestions. Hundreds of ideas were generated through this technique. Obviously, ideas resulting from brainstorming are just that — ideas in their rawest form. They do not represent actions that have been discussed or judged as to their relative effectiveness. Without now judging their merits or practicality, they are offered for critical consideration.

The following thirty actions were selected from those generated through brainstorming. Perhaps these and the other ideas which are listed in Appendix B, Numbers 1, 2, and 3, will serve as catalysts and springboards for action.

Relating Community to School

Provide various kinds of learning opportunities at school centers for community members of all ages and interests;

Utilize community members of various ages and backgrounds as classroom resource people to share their knowledge, skills and experiences;

Involve the chamber of commerce and selected local governmental agencies in the development of a field-trip guide for classroom teachers;

Develop a "volunteers in education" program which utilizes community members of all ages to help school faculty provide various learning experiences;

Introduce two-directional adoption programs, such as "adopt a grandparent" and "adopt a classroom," into schools to provide opportunities for children and senior adults to enjoy and benefit from one another;

Diversify teacher load to include working directly with parents in parent-education learning opportunities;

Involve students and recent alumni in program evaluation in order to facilitate curriculum improvement;

Provide a system for continuous flow of information regarding community needs and concerns utilizing area representatives, organizations, community members and students;

Utilize school buses for transporting community members to and from education programs;

Utilize school facilities for town meetings and club and agency headquarters.

Relating School to Community

Establish release time for teachers to go out into the community and visit parents, homes and neighborhoods of youth in their classes;

Utilize foods prepared in school lunch centers and training facilities for "meals on wheels" types of programs for elder community members;

Develop a listing of agencies and businesses which are willing to accept students to work in internships or on a part-time basis with their organizations;

Utilize youth in functional roles with municipal agencies in order for them to become more aware of agency functions and services;

Utilize educational service teams and educational action teams consisting of people with varying backgrounds, ages and occupations to address identified community problems;

Involve professional people and organizations in acquiring curriculum materials and in curricular endeavors;

Provide incentives for community institutions and agencies to share and to build adjacent facilities, to share staff and financial resources;

Develop strong, effective, representative and functional community councils;

Extend educational programs and services to shut-ins, the incarcerated, and other confined persons;

Develop local park areas and school grounds utilizing community initiative and labor.

Affecting School Curriculum

Establish a standing curriculum innovations committee which would receive and process recommendations for curriculum change from interested people;

Discard the normal academic calendar and utilize facilities year-round with learning opportunities of varying lengths;

Encourage student-taught programs such as miniclasses;

Encourage experimentation wherein life concerns are taught as course subjects;

Provide basic learning experiences for all community members and promote awareness that such learning opportunities are available throughout a person's lifetime;

Involve people who will be affected by any educational changes throughout the process in order to gain their acceptance and assistance;

Involve community education leadership in curriculum planning and development;

Integrate K-12 and after-school administrative organization into a single unit;

Establish a clearinghouse for the management of volunteers, field trips and resource persons;

Explore cooperative educational endeavors among educational institutions such as public schools, community colleges and universities.

WHOSE RESPONSIBILITY?

This chapter has highlighted various resources for curriculum change. Existing resources have been identified, actions suggested, and leadership discussed in light of effectiveness. Now, who should be responsible for curriculum improvement?

It appears that any one of the resources thus identified can serve as an effective catalyst for curriculum change and, in combination with any others, can be even more effective. Thus it is the responsibility of every concerned individual and organization to attempt to improve curriculum.

A caution is sounded, however. People attempting to reconstruct curriculum must be careful to avoid a possessive attitude about their ideas or programs. Care must be taken to allow personal goals to become the goals of others. New advocates need to be welcomed and encouraged to draw their own interpretations. They should also be allowed to build upon the original ideas and programs, and share in ownership. With each additional advocate come new ideas, talents and commitment. Compromises may often be necessary.

Who should be responsible for curriculum improvement? *All of us!*

8. IT'S UP TO US

The democratic problem in education is not primarily a problem of training children; it is the problem of making a community within which children cannot help growing up to be democratic, intelligent, disciplined to freedom, reverent of the goods of life, and eager to share in the tasks of the age. A school cannot produce this result; nothing but a community can do so. Consequently, we can never be satisfied that we have met the educational problems of our day when we have good schools. We must have good communities.

— Joseph K. Kart, *The Discovery of Intelligence*

OUR NEW FRONTIER

We are now moving into Amercia's Third Frontier, observes Duane S. Elgin, a Stanford Research Institute social policy analyst. He suggests that as a people we are beginning to undergo a profound change in our perception of ourselves and of our world — "the opening of a new frontier."

America's first frontier was the fabled open land to the west. Our challenge was to settle a rich but harsh environment. The first frontier closed at the turn of this century, and a second — the industrial or technological — frontier opened to replace it. The challenge became mastery of the environment we had usurped in pursuit of material affluence. With some exceptions, that challenge has now been met. Today, as concern for the environment increases and we realize the limits of world resources, we are witnessing — symbolically at least — the closing of this second great frontier.

Even now, the new third frontier is opening. It is a frontier of social and individual change, the exact dimensions of which are still unclear but whose rough outline is discernible. It is the frontier of the person, exploring in community with others the next stage of human possibility. Challenges along our past frontiers were external: in one case, mastery of the land; in the second, manipulation of technology. The challenge of the third frontier is primarily an internal one — realizing our human collective potential.[1]

Those geographic and technological frontiers were relatively easy to pioneer and develop because their exploration and penetration were largely in tune with America's dominant value outlooks and convictions. But the new human frontier — this Third Frontier — is something else again. For it not only questions many of our historic values (such as constant unlimited economic growth, exploitation of natural resources for private profit, glorification of large families and the absolute sovereignty of nations), but it also demands fundamental political, economic, social and educational changes through community, national and world societies.

Whether we like it or not, profound social changes for better or worse are inevitable during the final quarter of this century. Many of us will be greatly disturbed by those changes, however imperative and constructive they may be. For most of us, when facing social change, react like the little old lady who said that nobody would get her up in one of those jet planes, no sir! Anytime she had to travel it would be the way God intended his creatures to get around — by train!

CHANGE AND COMMITMENT

Technological change is disturbing to many people, and social change, including educational change, even more so. For significant social change is usually perceived as a kind of personal threat, especially by those who are well fed, comfortable, established, and complacent. These people are not only the Archie Bunker types; they include board of education members, school administrators, classroom teachers, college faculty members, and service club leaders. Whether social change is the rise of Women's Liberation, emergence of avowed homosexuals, the coming of a new school superintendent, or some proposal for a drastically revised curriculum, we tend to be emotional, doubtful, even opposed, with sincere and convincing reasons, naturally. Almost always establishment persons tend to feel that the way things are, or were sometime ago, are the right ways, the normal ways, even the God-intended ways. It seems to be human nature to prefer the familiar to the innovative, the traditional to the novel, the solace of security to the challenge of change, for that's "the way it 'spozed to be."[2]

This personal tendency toward social and educational conformity is further compounded by the fact that organizations become institutionalized;

that is, set in their ways, satisfied with a degree of success, devoted to their usual patterns of operation, and resistant to marked changes in their designated policies, programs, and evaluation procedures. In a word, an established organization becomes an Establishment. In this development, schools and colleges are no exception.

As a profession and as individuals in it, educators are pretty well established. Despite their sincere intentions and genuine commitment to education, they are inclined to feel that the familiar goals and curriculum, hence the comfortable aspects of our institutions, are basically sound and valid, and will remain adequate if only they are updated a bit here and there and if more money is found to meet the budget.

But they are also aware in their candid moments that no society, community, school or college ever stands still. Constant social change is always inherent in both technological advance and human relationships. As a result, some sociological indigestion, even cultural convulsions, are to be expected in all communities large and small, urban and rural, progressive and backward.

Educators know, too, that the whole history of education is the story of how old complacencies have been uprooted by new conditions of life. Ever since Socrates, educational reformers have shown that major changes in human society produce new and insistent human needs and that these emergent needs make imperative new and often startling philosophies, processes and programs in education.

Confronted by the ever-changing educational needs of our times, some people reactively try to *ignore change* as being of no concern to them. Either they say "so what?" and accept minor changes with indifference, or they timidly close their eyes to the whole scene and whisper that "we have no problems here — let's not stir up trouble." They may agree that much is wrong with society and the schools, and that "somebody should do something," but personally they do not want to get too involved. They seem to assume, as did the proverbial ostrich, that if you just don't look now the whole problem will somehow go away. But it probably will not!

Other people *resist change*, especially in basic curriculum design, as something inherently unwarranted, undesirable, dangerous, and not even to be seriously considered. They may agree that in the long run drastic curriculum revision is needed, but they do not intend to let their well-established and therefore psychologically secure practices be altered very much. They just quietly dig in their heels, saying, "We're going to keep things the way they have been." Or they may rant about outside agitators, troublemakers, educational do-gooders, thus dismissing all new ideas because of their prejudice against the source. Such people often get trapped by their own prejudices because change does come and, in its coming, often overrides them harshly.

Still others merely *accept change* if and when it comes upon them. They do not ignore it or resist it; they just passively take what comes and make the best of the situation at that time. Mildly forward-looking they may be, but that is enough for them. They ride with the tide, whether it flows or ebbs; they roll with the punches whatever their source; they do not really care what happens as long as they can stay on top of the situation. Whatever else they may be, they are not the educational statespersons so desperately needed today.

But fortunately there are other folks who are imaginative, courageous and dynamic. They are the hope for a better future. They take the lead to *assist change* because they recognize that some changes, especially in curriculum structure, are long overdue. These leaders are willing, even eager, to look around themselves to identify needs and resources, to look back for helpful perspective on the present, and to look ahead to plan and help develop better education. They are well aware that drastic curriculum redesign is now clearly imperative. They are also ready to help develop through creative school and community cooperative efforts a new plan and organization. They know, too, that to assist needed change, to guide and implement that change, to keep it within the bounds of the democratic process, may well bring some tension, turmoil and conflict.

These are four basic attitudes toward social and educational change in general and toward curriculum reconstruction in particular. Is there any constructive value in any of the first three mentioned? Are they not the routes of educational stagnation, school and college failure, and youth betrayal? Is not the only creative and justifiable outlook that of assisting needed curriculum change as speedily and comprehensively as possible?

Those who are concerned about people and the future in this tumultuous era will do well to ponder hard and long two demanding questions:

Without a truly functional, life-centered curriculum to build soundly the foundations for better living, are not children, youth and adults hapless victims of educational failure?

Shall we now move ahead with comprehensive community education to design and develop life-centered learning to meet the individual and societal needs of a new era?

In education as in religion there are both priestly and prophetic stances. The priestly posture looks ever backward for present direction: to tradition, precedent, dogma, and hallowed ritual. But the prophetic poise is forward, accepting the challenge of change to meet new needs produced by new conditions of life. The prophet finds in the past, helpful perspective, but not restrictive controls. In the present are the urgent concerns and creative resources. And from a guiding vision of a better human future, the prophet draws warm and vibrant inspiration for the urgent tasks of the new age.

In America's first century James Russell Lowell, poet, critic, and diplomat, observed that:

> New occasions teach new duties; time makes ancient good uncouth;
> They must upward still, and onward, who would keep abreast of truth;
> Lo, before us gleam her campfires! We ourselves must Pilgrims be,
> Launch our Mayflower, and steer boldly through the desperate winter sea,
> Nor attempt the future's portal with the past's blood-rusted key.[3]

That is our challenge now, for America's Third Century!

It is never enough to imitate the best of the past, to recite, however glibly, the wisdom of those who have led us to the present.

Our job now is to follow their guiding stars into new lands, not to rest content by the ashes of their dying campfires.

If we share their vision, even in part, let us in dedication and with renewed vigor stride forward to build ever better the learnings and so the lives of all people, now and for the years to come.

APPENDIX A

Community Education Directory

Number 1
Overview of National Status

Number of school districts implementing community education	1185 *
Number of community-school centers in operation (Buildings)	5062 *
Approximate number of persons enrolled in community education related activities per year	4,339,111 †
Weekly average number of participants in community education related activities, excluding enrollments	2,172,468 †
Average number of institutions and agencies cooperating with each school district	15 †
Number of community and junior colleges providing community service activities	500
Number of states with community education legislation enacted	11
Number of states with community education staff personnel at state department of education level	27
Number of states currently planning for community education personnel at state department of education level	11
Number of university and college centers for community education development	80

*as of 31 March 1975

†as of June 30, 1976

Note: Information collected from National Community Education Association, National Center for Community Education, Charles Stewart Mott Foundation, and American Association of Community and Junior Colleges.

Number 2
Status at the State Level

State	Community Education legislation enacted	Community Education legislation pending	Existing C.E. position	Projected and planning for staff development
Alabama			X	
Alaska	X		X	
Arizona		X		
Arkansas				X
California				X
Colorado	X		X	
Connecticut			X	
Delaware				
Florida	X		X	
Georgia	X			X
Hawaii				
Idaho				
Illinois		X	X	
Indiana			X	
Iowa				X
Kansas				
Kentucky			X	
Louisiana			X	
Maine			X	
Maryland	X		X	
Massachusetts	X			
Michigan	X		X	
Minnesota	X		X	
Mississippi				
Missouri		X	X	
Montana				
Nebraska				X
Nevada		X	X	
New Hampshire				
New Jersey			X	
New Mexico				
New York				
North Carolina				X
North Dakota				X
Ohio			X	
Oklahoma				
Oregon		X	X	
Pennsylvania			X	
Rhode Island				
South Carolina		X	X	
South Dakota				X
Tennessee				X
Texas			X	
Utah	X		X	
Vermont			X	
Virginia			X	
Washington	X		X	
W. Virginia		X	X	
Wisconsin				X
Wyoming				X
Washington, D.C.	X		X	

Number 3
Federal Legislation

President Gerald R. Ford, in one of his first acts as President, signed the Education Amendments Act, P. L. 93-380, in August 1974. Community education was a component of that act.

In recognition of the fact that the school, as the prime educational institution of the community, is most effective when the school involves the people of that community in a program designed to fulfill their education needs, and that Community Education promotes a more efficient use of public education facilities through an extension of school buildings and equipment, it is the purpose of this section to provide educational, recreational, cultural, and other related community services, in accordance with the needs, interests, and concerns of the community, through the establishment of the Community Education program as a center for such activities in cooperation with other community groups.[1]

The legislation defined a "Community Education program" as:

. . . a program in which a public building, including but not limited to a public elementary or secondary school or community or junior college, is used as a community center operated in conjunction with other groups in the community, community organizations, and local governmental agencies, to provide educational, recreational, cultural, and other related community services for the community that center serves in accordance with the needs, interests, and concerns of that community. Nothing in this section shall be construed to prohibit any applicant under this section from carrying out any activity with funds derived from other sources.[2]

In order to carry out the purposes and provisions of this legislation, the United States Commissioner of Education was authorized to make grants to state and local educational agencies to pay the federal share of the cost of planning, establishing, expanding, and operating community education programs. The Commissioner was authorized to expend for the purposes of state educational agencies and local educational agencies the sum of $15 million for each fiscal year prior to 1 July 1978. (The Ford Administration had requested $3,553,000 for fiscal year 1976.)

The federal share of said programs would be as follows:

80% of a program to establish a new community education program;

65% of a program to expand or improve a community education program for the first year in which such a program is assisted under this section, and 55% in any fiscal year thereafter;

40% of a program to maintain or carry out a community education program.

In order to assure proper application, the legislation states:

The Commissioner shall not approve an application submitted by a local educational agency unless the State educational agency of the State in which that local educational agency is located has been given an opportunity to review, and make comment on, such application.[3]

The Commissioner was authorized to make grants to institutions of higher education to develop and establish or expand programs which will train persons to plan and operate community education programs. The Commissioner was authorized to expend the sum of two million dollars for each fiscal year ending prior to 1 July 1978 for the purposes of higher education training. (As of press time, this amount has been reduced considerably since only $3,553,000 was requested for fiscal year 1976 by the Ford Administration for all aspects of Act P. L. 93-380.)

The federal legislation also authorized the Commissioner to establish or designate a clearinghouse to gather and disseminate information received from community education programs, including, but not limited to, information regarding new programs, methods to encourage community participation, and ways of coordinating community education programs with other community services. Another provision of the legislation authorized the Commissioner to establish an eleven-member advisory council to advise the Commissioner on policy matters relating to the interests of community schools.

Finally, the legislation authorized the Commissioner to insure that there be equitable geographical distribution of community education programs throughout the United States in both urban and rural areas.

This federal legislation is important and has potential for contributing significantly to the growth of community education in our nation. Caution must be taken, however, to insure the investment of these monies in good community education endeavors, not in merely "dressed up" forms of non-community related programs. Care must be taken not to allow actions that might contribute to the adulteration or prostitution of the genuine community education concept.

Those who wish to examine the federal legislation more closely may request a copy of it from any Center for Community Education Development or directly from the Director of the Office of Community Education, United States Office of Education, Department of Health, Education and Welfare, Washington, D.C. 20202

Number 4
National Community Education Association

The National Community Education Association was founded in 1966 with approximately two hundred charter members. The organization was designed for the "improvement and expansion of the community school philosophy as an integral and necessary part of the educational process." Two years later the Board of Directors adopted an official statement clarifying the purposes they sought:

> Community School Education is a comprehensive and dynamic approach to pubic education. It is a philosophy that pervades all segments of educational programming and directs the thrust of each of them toward

the needs of the community. The community school serves as a catalytic agent by providing leadership to mobilize community resources to solve identified community problems. This marshalling of all forces in the community helps to bring about change as the school extends itself to all people. Community School Education either affects all children, youth and adults directly or it helps to create an atmosphere and environment in which all men (sic) find security and self-confidence, thus enabling them to grow and mature in a community which sees its schools as an integral part of community life.

The Association has contributed significantly to the growth of community education and has played a major role in the passage of federal legislation. Most recently, the Association developed the National Community Education Information Clearinghouse, a retrieval and dissemination center for information on community education. The Clearinghouse makes available, upon request, all past and current research in the field, dissertations and theses on community education, training and curriculum designs, program evaluation designs, bibliographies, a newsletter file, magazine articles, plus other useful materials. Special searches for requested information are provided through the computer data bank. The Clearinghouse also publishes a *Research Bulletin* bimonthly which briefly reports completed research in community education.

Number 5
State and Regional Associations

The following state and regional associations have been organized to promote community education.

Alabama Community Education Association

Arizona Community Education Association

California Community Education Association

Colorado Association of Community Educators

Florida Association of Community Educators

Hawaii Community Education Association

Massachusetts Community School League, Incorporated

Michigan Community School Education Association

Mid-America Community Education Association

Minnesota Community Education Association

New Jersey Association for Community Education

Pennsylvania Community Education Association

Ohio Community School Education Association

Oregon Community Education Association

Tennessee Community Education Association

Texas Community Education Association

Number 6
Centers for Community Education

Community education has grown significantly since 1966 and continues to grow, due greatly to leadership provided by numerous centers for community education. As of now, some seventy-one centers located at universities, colleges, and state departments of education provide, at no cost to the recipients, consultation and training services to public schools, community colleges, universities, and other educational agencies located in communities throughout the nation. Assistance provided by the centers includes: 1) information on community education; 2) consultant help in developing and implementing community education; 3) ideas for securing financial assistance; 4) aid in securing and training community education personnel; 5) preservice and inservice educational opportunities; 6) evaluation of community education; 7) university credit course work in community education; and 8) information on additional consultant services available.

Funding for most of these centers is shared between the respective institutions, local sources of revenue, and the Charles Stewart Mott Foundation of Flint, Michigan. The Mott Foundation has indeed served as a catalyst and facilitator for significant growth of community education.

The following is a listing of current Centers for Community Education.

CENTERS FOR COMMUNITY EDUCATION

ALABAMA
Alabama State Department of Education
111 Coliseum Boulevard
Montgomery, Alabama 36104

Center for Community Education
University Station
University of Alabama in Birmingham
Birmingham, Alabama 35294

ALASKA
Alaska Center for Community Education
Alaska State Department of Education
State Office Building, Pouch F
Juneau, Alaska 99811

ARIZONA
Southwest Regional Center for Community School Development
415 Farmer Education Building
Arizona State University
Tempe, Arizona 85281

ARKANSAS
Community Education Development and Training Center
Graduate Education Building, Room 214
University of Arkansas
Fayetteville, Arkansas 72701

CALIFORNIA
California Regional Center for Community Education Development
Room 219, School of Education
California State University, San Jose
San Jose, California 95114

Community Education
Los Angeles County Education Center
9300 E. Imperial Highway
Downey, California 90242

California Center for Community Education Development
Department of Education, San Diego County
6401 Linda Vista Road
San Diego, California 92117

Center for Community Education
Santa Barbara Office of Education
P.O. Box 6307
Santa Barbara, California 93111

Center for Community Education
Agriculture & Environmental Sciences
University of California at Davis
Davis, California 95616

Center for Community Education
School of Education
University of Redlands
Redlands, California 92373

COLORADO

Community Education Center
Colorado Department of Education
Sherman at Colfax
Denver, Colorado 80203

Community Education Center
Colorado State University
Fort Collins, Colorado 85021

CONNECTICUT

Northeast Community Education Development Center
University of Connecticut, U-142
Storrs, Connecticut 06268

DELAWARE

Center for Community Education
College of Education
University of Delaware
Newark, Delaware 19711

DISTRICT OF COLUMBIA

Center for Community Education
American Association of Community and Junior Colleges
One Dupont Circle, N.W.
Suite 410
Washington, D.C. 20036

Center for Community Education
Gallaudet College
7th & Florida Avenue, N.E.
Washington, D. C. 20002
(Specialized Center working with Deaf and Hearing Impaired)

Center for Community Education
415 12th Street, N.W.
Presidential Building, Suite 1001
Washington, D.C. 20004

FLORIDA

Southeastern Regional Center for Community Education
College of Education, 106
Florida Atlantic University
Boca Raton, Florida 33432

Center for Community Education
College of Education
258 Norman Hall
University of Florida
Gainesville, Florida 32601

Center for Community Education
University of West Florida
Pensacola, Florida 32504

GEORGIA

Coastal Area Teacher Education Service Agency
Landrum Center, Box 8143
Georgia Southern College
Statesboro, Georgia 30458

HAWAII

Refer to California State Univ., San Jose

ILLINOIS
Center for Community Education
Illinois Community College Board
544 Iles Park Place
Springfield, Illinois 62718

Center for Community Education
Illinois Office of Education
100 North First Street
Springfield, Illinois 62706

Center for Community Education
College of Education, Ed. Adm.
Foundation Department
322 Wham
Southern Illinois University
Carbondale, Illinois 62901

General Office Building, Box 10
Southern Illinois University
Edwardsville, Illinois 62026

INDIANA
Institute for Community Education
Development
222 N. College
Ball State University
Muncie, Indiana 47306

Center for Community Education
Indiana State Department of Public
Instruction
120 W. Market Street, 10th Floor
Department of Public Instruction
Indianapolis, Indiana 46204

KANSAS
Center for Community Education
Development
201 Holton Hall, College of
Education
Kansas State University
Manhattan, Kansas 66506

KENTUCKY
Division of Community Education
Development
Bureau of Instruction
Kentucky Department of Education
Frankfort, Kentucky 40601

Center for Community Education
UPO — 1344
Morehead State University
Morehead, Kentucky 40351

LOUISIANA
Louisiana Center for Community
Education
Southeastern Louisiana University
Box 792, University Station
Hammond, Louisiana 70401

MAINE
Community Education Development
Center
138 Shibles Hall
University of Maine
Orono, Maine 04473

MARYLAND
Community Education Center
Maryland State Department of
Education
P.O. Box 8717 B.W.I. Airport
Baltimore, Maryland 21240

Center for Community Education
℅ Dept. of Recreation
University of Maryland
College Park, Maryland 20742

MASSACHUSETTS
Community Education Development
Center
Worcester State College
251 Salisbury Street
Worcester, Massachusetts 01609

MICHIGAN
Regional Center for Community
Education
Alma College
Alma, Michigan 48801

Center for Community Education
109 Ronan Hall
Central Michigan University
Mt. Pleasant, Michigan 48858

Center for Community Education
101 Boone Hall
Eastern Michigan University
Ypsilanti, Michigan 48197

Associate Community School
Director Program
Mott Community College
1401 E. Court Street
Flint, Michigan 48503

Center for Community Education
Learning Resources 102
Northern Michigan University
Marquette, Michigan 49855

Community School Development
Center
3314 Sangren Hall
Western Michigan University
Kalamazoo, Michigan 49001

MINNESOTA
Community Education Center
Box 4004
College of St. Thomas
St. Paul, Minnesota 55105

MISSISSIPPI
Center for Community Education
Dept. of Educational Administration
University of Southern Mississippi
Southern Station
Hattiesburg, Mississippi 39401

MISSOURI
Midwest Community Education
Development Center
Lucas Hall, Room 543
University of Missouri
St. Louis, Missouri 63121

MONTANA
Refer to Oregon, University of

College of Education
Montana State University
Bozeman, MT 59730

NEBRASKA
Center for Community Education
Henzlik Hall, 61-D
University of Nebraska
Lincoln, Nebraska 68508

NEVADA
Southern Nevada Office
Nevada State Department of
Education
Dawson Building
4055 S. Spencer, Suite 234
Las Vegas, Nevada 89109

NEW HAMPSHIRE
Refer to Connecticut, University of

NEW JERSEY
Bureau of Adult, Continuing and
Community Education
3535 Quakerbridge Road
P.O. Box 3181
Trenton, New Jersey 08619

Community Education Development
Center
14 Normal Avenue
Montclair State College
Upper Montclair, New Jersey 07043

NEW MEXICO
Community Education Center
New Mexico State University, Las
Cruces
Las Cruces, New Mexico 88003

NEW YORK
Center for Community Education
Area of Educational Administration
and Supervision
Syracuse University
103 Waverly Street
Syracuse, New York 13210

NORTH CAROLINA
Center for Community Education
Department of Administration and
Higher Education
Appalachian State University
Boone, North Carolina 28608

Center for Community Education
North Carolina State Department of Public Instruction
Raleigh, North Carolina 27611

NORTH DAKOTA
Center for Community Education
Department of Education
North Dakota State University
Fargo, North Dakota 58102

OHIO
Center for Community Education
407 Education Building
Kent State University
Kent, Ohio 44242

Center for Community Education Development
354 McGuffey Hall
Miami University
Oxford, Ohio 45056

Dept. of Personnel, Publications and Legal Services
Ohio State Department of Education
Ohio Department Building, Room 802
65 S. Front Street
Columbus, Ohio 43215

Center for Community Education
Wright State University
W 476 Millett
Dayton, Ohio 45431

OKLAHOMA
Community Education Center
309 Gundersen Hall
Oklahoma State University
Stillwater, Oklahoma 74074

OREGON
Northwest Community Education
Development Center
1724 Moss Street
University of Oregon
Eugene, Oregon 97403

PENNSYLVANIA
Educational Development Center
Shippensburg State College
Shippensburg, Pennsylvania 17257

Center for Community Education
School of Education
Indiana University of Pennsylvania
Indiana, Pennsylvania 15701

RHODE ISLAND
Community Education Development Center
Department of Administration & Curriculum
Rhode Island College
600 Mount Pleasant Avenue
Providence, Rhode Island 02908

SOUTH CAROLINA
Division of Adult Education
South Carolina State Dept. of Education
Rutledge Building
Columbia, South Carolina 29201

Center for Community Education
College of Education
University of South Carolina
Columbia, South Carolina 29208

SOUTH DAKOTA
Community School Development Center
School of Education
University of South Dakota
Vermillion, South Dakota 57069

TENNESSEE
Center for Community Education
Division of Education
The University of Tennessee at Nashville
323 McLemore Street
Nashville, Tennessee 37203

TEXAS
Center for Community Education
College of the Mainland
8001 Palmer Highway
Texas City, Texas 77590

Center for Community Education
College of Education
Texas A&M University
College Station, Texas 77843

UTAH
Rocky Mountain Regional Center for Community Education
281 Richards Building
Brigham Young University
Provo, Utah 84602

Center for Community Education
Utah State Department of Education
248 E. 500 South
Salt Lake City, Utah 84111

VERMONT
Community Education Development Center
College of Education
University of Vermont
Burlington, Vermont 05401

VIRGINIA
Mid-Atlantic Center for Community Education
University of Virginia, School of Education
Charlottesville, Virginia 22903

Cooperative Extension Center for Community Education
4078 Derring Hall
Virginia Polytechnic Institute & State University
Blacksburg, Virginia 24061

Center for Community Education
% Division of Secondary Education
Virginia State Department of Education
P.O. Box 6Q
Richmond, Virginia 23219

WASHINGTON
Center for Community Education Development
Old Capitol Building
Office of the State Superintendent of Public Instruction
Olympia, Washington 98504

WEST VIRGINIA
Center for the Study of Community Education
West Virginia College of Graduate Studies
Institute, West Virginia 25112

Community Education
Building 6, Room B-243
State Capitol Complex
1900 Washington Street, East
Charleston, West Virginia 25305

WISCONSIN
Refer to Michigan, Western Michigan Univ.

WYOMING
Wyoming Center for Community Education
School Services, College of Education
University of Wyoming
Laramie, Wyoming 82070

Number 7
The National Center for Community Education

Another organization, which has contributed greatly to the growth of community education, is the National Center for Community Education. The National Center, located in Flint, Michigan, is a consortium of universities and colleges working together to provide specialized training for potential community education leaders. The Center is an outgrowth of the Mott Inter-University Clinical Preparation Program and has for the past eleven years provided multiple internship experiences. The program has been highly successful, with hundreds of its graduates currently occupying major community education leadership roles throughout the nation. The Center changed its focus in 1974 from a year-long training endeavor to one of providing concentrated workshops of varying lengths for potential leaders identified by the regional centers. The programs offered at the National Center for Community Education are designed to complement training endeavors of the regional centers.

Number 8
International Association of Community Educators

The International Association of Community Educators was formally established at the Second Annual International Community Education Conference in Juarez, Mexico. Its purposes are to:

Provide a public forum for the free interchange and intercommunication of ideas and human-community development techniques and programs;

Encourage understanding and appreciation of the diverse cultures in the world, on the part of all people;

Provide a forum where any nation, organization, or institution may present a model for individual or community betterment so that other individuals, organizations or institutions may benefit from the initial work;

Encourage the understanding and employment of the basic fundamentals of community education;

To make maximum use of all community resources,

To encourage cooperation and coordination among individuals, groups and organizations to avoid unnecessary duplication of services and efforts,

To encourage citizen participation in both education and community affairs,

To develop programs and processes that can identify individual and community and world needs and assist in the successful attack on these problems,

To provide an opportunity for all organizations, institutions or groups to meet together in a concerted, cooperative attack on the unprecedented problems endangering the finite world from enjoying the benefits of peace, prosperity and progress for all its inhabitants.

APPENDIX B

BRAINSTORMING SESSIONS

Number 1 Ways To Relate Community Members and Resources with the Use of School Facilities and Instructional Endeavors

Number 2 Ways To Relate School Instructional Endeavors with the Community

Number 3 Ways To Directly Affect School Curriculum

The following ideas were generated through brainstorming. They do not represent actions that have been discussed or judged as to their relative effectiveness. Each is offered as grist for the mill in the discussion and planning of curriculum reconstruction directed towards life-concerns education. The authors' sincere thanks go to the following people for their energetic participation in the brainstorming sessions:

William Armstrong
William Blackwood
Willie Brennon
Nancy Dean
A. L. (Skip) Little
A. L. Stefurak
Stephen Taber
Katherine Watson
Pamela Zimpfer

Number 1
Ways To Relate Community Members and Resources with the Use of School Facilities and Instructional Endeavors

Use schools as centers for community activities such as meetings, exhibits and special programs.

Conduct seminars for parents which are designed to assist them in helping their children with school work.

Develop and maintain a current listing of community agencies, their respective services, and procedures for securing such services.

Provide inservice training for teachers involving business people as resources in order for them to communicate directly their employment needs and express possibilities for cooperation.

Provide incentives to encourage public service institutions to build adjacent to one another or share facilities in order to encourage interagency cooperation and facilitate referrals and team approaches.

Provide multi-age recreational opportunities at school centers and other public and private facilities.

Eliminate age perimeters for curricular activities.

Provide learning opportunities which focus on community history and leadership, utilizing community members as resource persons.

Provide learning opportunities which feature music, dance, customs, fashions, foods, artifacts and ways of life of people of various countries.

Provide opportunity for older students to serve as a big brother or sister in tutoring younger students.

Encourage experimental programs which require parent involvement for child participation.

Provide preservice and inservice training for teachers utilizing business and agency personnel as resource people in order for them to directly communicate their needs and possibilities for cooperative involvement.

Develop functional community councils, representative of the community, which will address themselves to the total curriculum of a school.

Involve community councils in need and goal identification, school staff selection, budget preparation, curriculum planning, facility planning and program evaluation.

Identify retired citizens who are willing to serve as a resource for instructional endeavors.

Provide and disseminate media materials which communicate services available from community institutions and agencies.

Build schools and acquire furniture which will accommodate people of varying ages and sizes.

Build or modify school buildings to accommodate people with handicaps.

Utilize school facilities as a gallery to exhibit arts and crafts created by community members.

Recognize parent and community member involvement via recognition banquets, awards, bulletin boards, etc.

Utilize community members to share their knowledge and skills of forgotten trades.

Number 2
Ways To Relate School Instructional Endeavors with the Community

Emphasize school faculty member participation on community planning and service committees.

Utilize minibuses and car shuttles to take small groups on field visitations.

Solicit volunteers who could be utilized at their job sites to assist in career awareness.

Develop procedures for cooperating with agencies who are willing to allow students to work on a part-time basis or intern with their organizations.

Train students in food preparation and use the food for a "meals on wheels" program for home and community members.

Pay teachers on a twelve-month basis and arrange for them to participate with other community agencies for portions of their assignment.

Provide opportunity for students to teach crafts and other leisure activities to community members who are homebound and convalescing.

Encourage business, industrial, governmental and church leaders to release space for various learning experiences.

Develop a system for students to volunteer their services into the community.

Increase "classrooms on wheels" activities which bring learning opportunities directly to the people.

Utilize school-age children and other community members to serve as readers and interpreters for persons with sight and hearing impairments.

Provide social studies and other such credit for structured community service work.

Maximize the use of public and private facilities to provide credit and non-credit program offerings for community members of all ages.

Provide daytime school learning opportunities out in the community.

Increase utilization of Junior Achievement types of programs which encourage small business development and association with existing business people.

Design school centers which do not accommodate all students at one time, thus encouraging alternative scheduling and utilization of the community itself for structured learning experiences.

Utilize a payment system in apprenticeship programs so that both employes and employers see monetary value of such programs.

Provide learning experiences for faculty, staff and community members that will broaden perceptions regarding communities and educational institutions and the potential for them to work more closely with one another.

Maximize the use of the community as a classroom.

Emphasize practical consumer education through utilization of local businesses and analysis of buyer behavior.

Provide training experiences for faculty to assist them in identifying community resources for their instructional endeavors.

Identify agencies who are willing to accept students to work in supervised internships or on a part-time basis.

Involve business and civic groups in programs and activities for youth.

Encourage participation in community bands, choirs and theaters.

Provide workshops for faculty to become aware of functions and services of community agencies.
Encourage team teaching, utilizing both professional teachers and lay citizens.
Provide learning opportunities in multi-dwelling units such as dormitories, apartments, and senior citizen housing areas.
Provide family programs and activities.
Involve community members at large in providing input in school endeavors through breakfast meetings, luncheons, coffee hours and other such activities.
Utilize long-time citizens to orient faculty on community history and leadership.
Support recurring annual events which have significance to the community.
Provide opportunity for teacher home visitations.
Encourage board of education and administrators to hold neighborhood meetings.
Provide a system and promote the knowledge of the system for student voluntary opportunities.
Involve students in voter registration, campaign awareness activities and in voting.

Number 3
Ways To Directly Affect School Curriculum

Provide year-round school programming utilizing systems such as the 45-15 and quinsemester plans.
Encourage utilization of community members or faculty on a one-to-one or small group basis to match excelling students with skilled persons, i.e., math student with local mathematician, science student with laboratory technician.
Utilize parent-teacher organizations and community councils to assist school faculty in greater use of community for all its instructional endeavors.
Decentralize authority and leadership in school systems.
Provide learning experiences and programs via themes rather than subject areas.
Provide problem-solving techniques throughout the instructional program to enable individuals to dissect a major problem into its components and address themselves to these components.
Encourage student taught programs in miniclasses.
Develop procedures for continued evaluation and modification of the total curriculum.

Request assistance from professional and skilled people to assist in curriculum material development.
Encourage application of subject matter and de-emphasize need for memorization of specific facts.
Encourage student developed programs of instruction.
Expand use of independent studies to meet specific needs of students.
Eliminate mandatory attendance requirements and encourage drop-in and drop-out approach.
Provide opportunity and time for teachers to work with students and community members in the planning of instruction.
Encourage integrated extradisciplinary learning. Examples: dramatization and demonstration of the various functions of a ball or sphere, molecular structures, crystallization and the like serving as art forms, and the utilization of art to interpret world government.
Introduce sports and recreational activities of peoples from different cultures and geographic regions of the world.
Utilize secondary level youth as aides in elementary programs.
Utilize module systems for scheduling educational programs.
Encourage program development which provides multicultural learning experiences.
Involve school-age youth in educational experiences for students with special learning disabilities.
Increase emphasis on lifelong sports such as tennis, golf, bowling, jogging, handball, gymnastics, and dance.
Develop experimental teacher training programs mutually planned by teacher preparation institutions and public schools.
Encourage apprenticeship programs.
Promote educational programs which encourage students to perform in a job role while seeking their formal education.
Provide and promote a life-centered philosophy study at the secondary level, utilizing parents as teachers.
Utilize students as classroom resource people.
Utilize a competency based approach to the evaluation of students in basic reading, writing and mathematics skills.
Inform all faculty in writing of purposes of new programs in order for them to be able to communicate these with community members.
Develop experimental study units which are not confined to regular school hours or days.
Develop experimental programs which do not utilize conventional grade level designations.
Develop new criteria for the evaluation of educators and education institutions.
Utilize a competency based approach to basic studies in lieu of grades.

Emphasize value clarification and problem-solving at the later elementary and secondary levels.

Communicate the purposes of educational institutions and demonstrate how life concerns can be solved through political processes.

Emphasize the need for cooperative efforts among people to solve life concerns.

Increase awareness of and emphasis on training for nonprofessional jobs.

Emphasize throughout all career programs the importance of all occupations and skills for a successful society.

Encourage cross-disciplinary approaches to instruction.

Orient entire faculty to entire program and service endeavors.

Develop a staff advisory council to serve the faculty and to serve as a model for the establishment of future representative councils.

Build elements of community needs into the school curriculum.

Encourage teacher preparation institutions to incorporate principles of community education in their undergraduate and graduate education curricula.

Provide after school activities which would complement day school educational programs.

Expand use of media when field trips are impractical.

Utilize older youth in day care center activities and programs.

Encourage international and regional exchange programs for educational faculty.

Encourage student exchange programs such as rural-urban, regional, and international.

Establish and promote annual leadership workshops.

NAME INDEX

SUBJECT INDEX

FOOTNOTES

Chapter 1

[1] Santa Barbara Center for the Study of Democratic Institutions, *The Center Magazine,* September-October 1974.
[2] John H. Filer, from a DePauw University commencement speech quoted in *The National Observer,* 6 September 1975.
[3] Robert L. Heilbroner, *An Inquiry into the Human Prospect* (W. W. Norton and Company, 1974), pp. 57, 138, 61.
[4] Kenneth E. Boulding, quoted by Priscilla P. Griffith in Alvin Toffler, ed., *Learning for Tomorrow* (New York: Random House, 1974), p. 197.
[5] *The Oregonian,* 18 November 1974.
[6] Barbara Ward, *The New York Times,* 11 November 1966.
[7] Daniel Moynihan, quoted in *The Oregonian,* 13 October 1975. The Business Council is an organization of one hundred corporation executives.
[8] Margaret Mead, Address to the graduating class of Simmons College, Boston, Mass. quoted in *Parade,* 29 June 1975.
[9] *U. S. News & World Report,* 23 June 1975.
[10] Norman Cousins, "Who Owns the Ozone?," *Saturday Review/World,* 5 October 1974, p. 4.
[11] Arnold J. Toynbee, in the "Foreword," *A Pictorial Record* (New York: United Nations, 1952).
[12] Arnold J. Toynbee, *Change and Habit: The Challenge of Our Time.* (Oxford University Press, 1966), pp. 138-39.
[13] Alvin Toffler, *Eco-Spasm Report.* (Bantam Books, 1975), p. 3
[14] *Ibid.* pp. 104-105.
[15] Lawrence A. Cremin, Convocation Address quoted in *TC Today,* October 1974.
[16] Harold Taylor, from an address "The Teacher in the World," delivered in Chicago, Ill., 16 February 1967.
[17] *NEA Reporter,* January 1976.

Chapter 2

[1] *Education for American Life:* (McGraw-Hill, 1938), p. 4.
[2] New York State Commission on the Quality, Cost and Financing of Elementary and Secondary Education, *Report of the Commission,* Vol. 2: New York State, 1972.
[3] Frank Brown, ed., *The Reform of Secondary Education: Report to the Public and the Profession:* (McGraw-Hill, 1973), p. 188.
[4] James Cass, *Saturday Review/World,* 19 October 1974. The full, unpublished report is available through the ERIC data retrieval system.
[5] Kettering Foundation *The Adolescent, Other Citizens, and Their High Schools: The Report of Task Force '74* (McGraw-Hill, 1975) p. xvi.
[6] *Ibid.,* pp. xvii-xviii
[7] *Ibid.,* pp. 61-62.
[8] Robert Finch, "The Question of Relevancy," *The School and the Democratic Environment* (Columbia University Press, 1970), p. 21.
[9] John Bremer, "A Curriculum, A Vigor, A Local Abstraction," *The Center Forum,* a publication of the Center for Urban Education, 1 March 1969.
[10] John Holt as quoted in a press interview, *Bellevue* (Washington) *American,* 12 October 1974.
[11] Alvin Toffler, *Learning for Tomorrow: The Role of the Future in Education* (Random House, 1974).
[12] J. I. Simmons and Barry Winegard, *It's Happening* (Santa Barbara, Calif.: Marc-Laird Publications, 1966), p. 28.
[13] Letter from Douglas Olsen to his father, 1975.

[14] *Parade Magazine,* 21 September 1975.
[15] *The Oregonian,* 7 October 1975.
[16] American Association of School Administrators, *Schools for a New World* (Washington, D.C.: The Association, 1947), p. 67.

Chapter 3

[1] Portions of this chapter are reprinted or adapted from Edward G. Olsen et al., *School and Community* (Prentice-Hall, Inc., 1954), Used by permission.
[2] Peter of Blois, quoted in William H. Burton, *Introduction to Education* (New York: D. Appleton Century Co., 1934), p. 392.
[3] Jon Amos Comenius, *The Great Didactic,* 1632.
[4] Jean Jacques Rousseau, *Emile,* 1762.
[5] Johan Heinrich Pestalozi, *Diary.*
[6] Herbert Spencer, "What Knowledge Is of Most Worth?," *Westminster Review,* July 1859.
[7] Francis Parker, quoted by Harold Rugg and B. Marion Brooks, *Teacher in School* (World Book Company, 1950), p. 254.
[8] John Dewey, *School and Society* (Chicago: University of Chicago Press, 1899), p. 1.
[9] National Society for the Study of Education, *The Rural School as a Community Center* (The Society, 1911), p. 66.
[10] Joseph K. Hart, *Educational Resources of Village and Rural Communities* (The Macmillan Company, 1913), p. 9.
[11] Ellsworth Collings, *An Experiment with a Project Curriculum* (The Macmillan Company, 1923), and *Junior-Senior Clearinghouse,* March 1935.
[12] Elsie Clapp, *Community Schools in Action* (Viking Press, 1939) p. 89.
[13] Glenn Kendall, "The Norris Educational Program," *Curriculum Journal,* March 1939.
[14] Richard C. Pendell, "A Final Interview with Frank Manley," *Community Education Journal,* November 1972.
[15] Paul R. Hanna, *Youth Serves the Community* (D. Appleton-Century Company, 1936), p. 21.
[16] American Association of School Administrators and the National Education Association, *Joint Statement on Purposes of Education in American Democracy,* pp. 50, 72, 90, 109, and passim.
[17] Samuel Everett, ed., *The Community School* (Appleton-Century Company, 1938), pp. 435-57 and passim.
[18] Quoted in Edward G. Olsen et al., *School and Community* (Prentice-Hall, 1954), pp. 516-17.
[19] American Association of School Administrators and the National Education Association, *Education for All American Youth* (The Associations, 1944).
[20] Edward G. Olsen, "Washington State's New Program," *Progressive Education,* January 1947.
[21] Edward G. Olsen et al., *School and Community* (Prentice-Hall, 1945, 1954), preface.
[22] National Society for the Study of Education, *The Community School* (Chicago: University of Chicago Press, 1953).
[23] Edward G. Olsen *The Modern Community School* (Appleton-Century-Crofts, 1953).
[24] Ernest O. Melby, *Administering Community Education* (Prentice-Hall, 1955), p. 167.
[25] *Foundations of Curriculum Making,* p. 14.
[26] *Social Services and the Schools,* pp. 60-61.
[27] *Teachers For Our Times,* p. 136.
[28] *Schools for a New World,* pp. 220, 101.
[29] *Toward Better Teaching,* p. 193.
[30] *Strengthening Community Life: Schools Can Help,* p. 15.
[31] *The Superintendent as Instructional Leader,* p. 93.
[32] Mary Conway Kohler, *Resources for Youth Newsletter,* 15 March 1975.

[33] *National Advisory Commission on Civil Disorders Report* (Bantam Books, 1968), p. 451.
[34] *Community Education Journal,* February 1971.
[35] Statement adopted by the National PTA Board of Managers, as reported in *National Community School Education Association News,* December 1971.
[36] *Community Education Journal,* May 1972.
[37] *Community Education Journal,* May-June 1974.
[38] *Paths to Better Schools* (National Education Association, 1945) p. 245.

Chapter 4

[1] Jack D. Minzey and Clyde LeTarte, *Community Education: From Program to Process* (Midland, Mich: Pendell Publishing Co., 1972), p. 3.
[2] Louis J. Tasse, "Schools for Everyone," *University of Miami Interaction,* Winter 1973.
[3] Committee on Human Resouces of the Metropolitan School Study Council, "Fifty Teachers to a Classroom" (The MacMillan Company, 1950).
[4] Edward G. Olsen, *School and Community Programs* (Prentice-Hall, 1949), Chapter 4; and *School and Community* (Prentice-Hall, 1954), Chapter 7.
[5] Maurice F. Seay, *Community Education: A Developing Concept* (Midland, Mich: Pendell Publishing Company, 1974), p. 19.
[6] Patsy Mink, "National Imperative," *Community Education Journal,* July-August 1974.
[7] V. M. Kerensky and Ernest O. Melby, *Education II — The Social Imperative,* (Midland, Mich: Pendell Publishing Company, 1971), p. 182.
[8] *Ibid.,* P. 182.
[9] National Community Education Association, *Membership Directory, 1975* (The Association).
[10] Howard W. Hickey, Curtis Van Voorhees, eds., *The Role of the School in Community Education* (Midland, Mich: Pendell Publishing Company, 1969), pp. 31-32.
[11] Jack D. Minzey and Clyde LeTarte, *Community Education: From Program to Process* (Midland, Mich: Pendell Publishing Company, 1972), p. 19.
[12] V. M. Kerensky, "The Definition Issue," *NCSEA News,* National Community School Education Association, May 1971.
[13] Donald C. Weaver, "Community Education — A Cultural Imperative," *The Community School and Its Administration* (Midland, Mich: Ford Press, Inc., January 1969).
[14] Maurice F. Seay et al., *Community Education: A Developing Concept* (Midland, Mich: Pendell Publishing Company, 1974), p. 11.
[15] V. M. Kerensky, "Community Education: A New Synergism," *Community Education Journal,* March-April 1974, p. 30.
[16] C. C. Peters, *Foundations of Educatioal Sociology* (New York: The MacMillan Company, 1963), p. 243.
[17] William A. Yeager, *Home-School-Community Relations* (Pittsburgh: University of Pittsburgh Press, 1939), pp. 3-4.
[18] Edward G. Olsen et al., *School and Community* (New York: Prentice-Hall, 1954), pp. 447, 448.
[19] Kerensky and Melby, op. cit., p. 165.

Chapter 5

[1] This proposal was first presented by Edward G. Olsen in *Community Education Journal,* February 1972, and in *Phi Delta Kappan,* November 1972.
[2] New York Museum of Modern Art, 1955.

[3] Alvin Toffler, *Learning for Tomorrow: The Role of the Future in Education* (Random House, 1974), p. 18.
[4] Alvin Toffler, quoted by James J. Morisseau in "The Future of Education," *Scholastic Teacher,* February 1974.
[5] Sydney J. Harris, "The Meaning of 'Relevant'," *San Francisco Sunday Examiner,* 9 January 1972. Reprinted by permission of Sydney J. Harris and Field Newspaper Syndicate.
[6] Eric Sevareid, from "Richard Nixon's Mandate," *Saturday Review,* 4 January 1969.
[7] Association for Supervision and Curriculum Development, *Action for Curriculum Improvement* (The Associated Press, 1951), p. 221.
[8] *Adult Education,* Thomas Y. Crowell, 1927, pp. 82-83.
[9] Chamberlin, Chamberlin, Drought and Scott, *Adventure in American Education,* Vol. IV (Harper & Brothers), pp. 41, 62, 172.
[10] Paul Hanna, "What Thwarts the Community School Curriculum?," *Community Education Journal,* May 1972.
[11] *Time,* 18 November 1974.
[12] Edward G. Olsen et al., *School and Community* (Prentice-Hall, 1954), pp. 81-82.
[13] This section originally appeared in Edward G. Olsen's "Is the Community School Anti-Intellectual?", *School Executive,* October 1958, and in *Education Digest,* December 1958.
[14] Maurice F. Seay, "The Catalyst and the Process of Community Education," *Community Education Journal,* November-December 1974.
[15] Clyde Campbell, *The Community School and Its Administrator* (Newsletter of the Mott Program of the Flint, Michigan, Board of Education) September 1969.
[16] Maurice F. Seay et al., *Community Education: A Developing Concept* (Midland, Mich: Pendell Publishing Company, 1974), p. 189.

Chapter 6

[1] Lao-Tse as quoted in George Seldes, *The Great Quotations* (Lyle Stuart, 1960), p. 398.
[2] Joseph Wittmer and Robert D. Myrick, *Facilitative Teaching: Theory and Practice* (Goodyear Publishing Company, 1974), pp. 40-49.
[3] J. William Pfeiffer and John E. Jones, eds., *Handbooks of Structured Experiences for Human Relations Training* and the *Annual Handbooks for Group Facilitators* (University Associates).
[4] Robert Chin, "Basic Strategies and Procedures in Effecting Change," *Planning and Effecting Changes in Education,* E. L. Morphet and Charles O. Ryan, eds. (Publishers Press, Inc., 1967).

Chapter 7

[1] *The Nature of the Curriculum for the 80's and Onwards,* published by O.E.C.D. Publications, 2 Rue Andre-Pascal, Paris-16e, No. 29553, 1972 as cited in *Education Today,* 1972.
[2] Institute for Responsivie Education, "Assistance for Alternative Schools," *Citizen Action in Education* (New Haven, Conn.: The Institute, Spring 1974), p. 9.

Chapter 8

[1] Duane S. Elgin, "America's Third Frontier," *Modern Maturity,* April-May 1975.

[2] The title of James Herndon's best-selling book on the classroom war behind the crisis in our schools. *The Way It 'Spozed to Be* (Bantam Books, 1965, 1968).
[3] James Russell Lowell, *The Present Crisis,* 1844.

Appendix A

[1] "U.S. Congress Passes First Federal Legislation to Support Community Education," *Community Education Journal,* September-October 1974.
[2] *Ibid.*
[3] *Ibid.*
[4] National Community Education Association, *Community with You Creates Us* (The Association, 1975).

NOTES

NOTES

NOTES